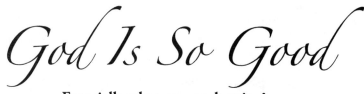

God Is So Good

Especially when you are hurting!

Dr. John Bishop
God Is So Good Ministries

SOLID ROCK PUBLICATIONS
600 Garland Ave. • Hot Springs, Arkansas 71913
www.solidrockpublications.com

Second Printing 2006

Copyright © 2004
by Solid Rock Publications
Hot Springs, Arkansas

Cover and Layout By Chantha Chhim

ISBN: 0-9741778-2-2

Printed in the United States of America

For booking information, please contact:
God Is So Good Ministries
99 Christian Ranch Road
Rose Bud, Arkansas 72137
(501)-556-5837

Dedication

*I think everybody knows to whom I would dedicate this
autobiography that recounts the wonderful grace and
goodness of God in my life since that difficult day in
1995, when I was diagnosed with meningitis.*

*I dedicate to my dearest friend on earth, my wife, whom
I lovingly call, "My Donna."*

*It is doubtful I would even be here today without her love,
patience, tenderness, and understanding. If I were here
without her, I certainly wouldn't have the joy and
happiness I have today.*

Donna, I love and adore you!

Moving to Murfreesboro!

Since the publishing of this book, my Donna and I have moved to the great Franklin Road Baptist Church in Murfreesboro, Tennessee. Dr. Mike Norris is the pastor at this wonderful church filled with some of the most loving and caring people you would ever meet. We still have our mobile home on the campgrounds of Triple "S" Christian Ranch there in Rose Bud, AR.

My family tells me that I started this camp thirty years ago (1975), and I sure am glad I did, even though I don't remember doing it! We can still be reached at the Rose Bud address and plan to spend our summers there teaching my class time as long as the Lord allows me to do so. I love kids. I think I love kids more now than I ever have! Teens and kids have been so accepting of me and my disabilities. I can just be myself around them and teach them truths that I pray will help them when tough times come into their lives.

My Donna and I wanted to focus more on our God Is So Good Ministries. Dr. Norris and I became close friends during the times I preached at the church there in Tennessee. Our hearts were so knit together. One reason is because of the health issues he has had to work through himself. In 1991, Dr. Norris was diagnosed with Systematic Active Rheumatoid Arthritis – a very crippling disease. I had tears as he told me of the time when he was so discouraged and in such pain that he felt like giving up. I have been at that point of discouragement many times as some of you have as well. At this time, Dr. Norris was practically bedfast and could only walk with the help of large doses of medication. One day, his dear wife Mila bent over him, and with hot tears dripping onto his face, she encouraged him to go on. He did, and we are all blessed! He and I have shared in God's command to "Rejoice with them that do rejoice, and weep with them that weep." (Romans 12:15) After reading this book, you can easily see some similarities in our situations. My Donna helped me to keep going even as "his Mila" urged him on.

I had the privilege of preaching on their 50th anniversary of the church, which was started by two of God's giants of Fundamentalism, Dr. Bill Rice and Dr. John R. Rice. We had a record-breaking day on that occasion that resulted in 2,679 people in attendance. Dr. Norris recorded 61 decisions for salvation, and many other special decisions were made at the altar that day. The spirit of the church and the Spirit of the Lord were so refreshing! In the last five years, I have only been in a handful of services like the one that day. I pray for more, and I am certain it is more my fault than anyone else's that I do not see more.

We didn't move to Murfreesboro just because we were so excited about a big day. We have had the privilege of being in several "big days" with churches around the country. They have all been exciting, although I must say there was something special about that day which stood out to both of us. We saw a great church with a history of some of America's greatest preachers moving even further into the future with an ever-expanding vision for God. This great pastor and people have a heart for souls and a passion for the hurting people of Murfreesboro and the world.

We are so excited about being a part of this and hope you will pray for us and with us as we go into the future with an even greater vision for the hurting people of this world. The **YES CLUBS INTERNATIONAL** program we started is reaching into public schools in several states now. I plan to have new books out soon along with the tracts designed to help those who are hurting or to help those who are working with those who are hurting. Many people would do more for the hurting if they just knew how, and I want to help them learn how.

If you would like to contact us, you may do so through the addresses listed below:

Evangelist John Bishop
99 Christian Ranch Road
Rose Bud, AR 72137
(501)556-5837

Franklin Road Baptist Church
3148 Franklin Road
Murfreesboro, TN 37128
(615) 890-0820

www.Godissogood.net

A Word from Pastor Mike Norris

What a blessing it has been to have Brother John and Mrs. Donna Bishop come to Murfreesboro, Tennessee! I am so grateful that the Lord has allowed our paths to cross again. When I was a teenager, he preached in our Church in West Virginia. He was a powerful preacher then, but since his illness, I believe the Lord is using him more now than ever. I think this is because of his ministry to hurting people. Someone has said, "A preacher will never want for a crowd if he preaches to broken hearts." This is the ministry of Brother John Bishop! He has a unique gift of encouraging the hurting and motivating them to rise above their circumstances in life.

Our people here at Franklin Road Baptist Church love the Bishops. Our teenagers and children love it when they can be in town. They always make their way through the school, speaking to our students, and they make it a point to attend ballgames. The Bishops enjoy going soulwinning with our people. He always says, "I'm looking for a hurting person behind each door." He has taught me that there are hurting people behind more doors than we realize. Because of our busy lifestyles we often pass them by.

Just like Brother Bishop, my health has improved, and I am so grateful. During the worst days of my illness, I made the decision that God was still good, even if I didn't get better. As hard as it may be to believe this, it is still true – God is always good! Brother Bishop has repeated this fact over and over in this book. If you are convinced of this great truth, may I encourage you to find a hurting person today and seek to be a blessing to them. If you are still struggling with this, may I close by saying, as lovingly as I know how, God is so good! I pray that you will begin to enjoy His goodness today!

Contents

Preface

*G*od's goodness became the theme of my life shortly after I was stricken with meningitis in October of 1995. Although it may seem strange to many people to make the onset of such a difficult illness the beginning of such an uplifting theme in my life, I think it is both fitting and understandable once you have read the rest of what has happened to me since that difficult day. That day in October when My Donna (I will explain why I refer to my wife as "My Donna" shortly.) took me to the little hospital in Heber Springs, Arkansas, became the first day of what have become God's greatest blessings in my life! What started as a terrible headache that still causes me pain has become a most unusual story of life and love! Don't put this book down, because you are going to love to read about God's goodness in a fresh and loving way!

The particular day she took me to the emergency room escapes my memory along with a lifetime of memories that were lost during my illness. I am relating to you in this book things that have happened to me since that day or what has been related to me by My Donna and others. I remember only little small segments of my original hospital stay. Little did My Donna and I know that this illness would start us on one of the most unusual and wonderful journeys we could imagine!

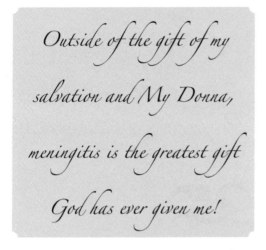

Outside of the gift of my salvation and My Donna, meningitis is the greatest gift God has ever given me!

Right there, that very day, began the first of innumerable good things God was about to do for me. He had on duty in the emergency room that day a man I truly believe is one of the finest Christian physicians a patient could ever ask for, Dr. Frank Bivins! He has given me the finest quality of health-care that could be given with the wonderful additions of Christian concern and grace. He helped me through some very difficult times of trials and severe pain. He even went to the point of being willing to visit my home to assist me through times of painful suffering! God has received much thanks for this dear man and his ministry! God always has the right person for His work! You will see this principle more than once in my life story.

I looked back at a letter addressed to a dear Christian I had written just about two years after my illness began. I kept a copy of the letter, which I many times do to remind me who I have written. I began the letter like this: "Two years ago my nightmare began..." If I were to write you a letter recounting my last seven years, I would begin my letter this way: "In October of 1995, my dream began..." Instead of the word *nightmare*, I would put *dream* because I feel like my life since then has been more like a dream come true than a nightmare that you hope will soon end. I think you'll agree when we laugh, cry, and recount the many wonderful things God has brought out of such strange circumstances.

My greatest desire will be that everyone who reads this biography will think and say one thing when they finish: "The Lord sure is good! Only a good God could do all that!" If that happens, I will rejoice, and I would love to hear from you because that keeps my spirits up on my "not-so-good" days of pain. Notice I didn't say "bad" days! At one time I would have said "bad" days, but now I even consider the days of suffering as beneficial and helpful to me. Now I describe all my days this way: "good days" and "not-so-good days."

This project of writing an autobiography has been a long, difficult task, but I have been motivated by my family and friends to do so. I will include some of my failures (warts) along with many small victories I have enjoyed these past years. Truth is, I will probably include a few more of my weaknesses than my family would. I will also include some of my "past" life, which is how I describe my life before meningitis. Many people have expressed an interest in that time period of my life.

This book first started by using a software program in which I could talk and the computer would type my words. My Donna bought that for me since I had to type most things several times before it made much sense. Even after I have finished, it is questionable how much sense it makes! After a computer crash and countless other delays brought on by my ignorance and mis-handling, here is the finished product. I hope you feel it was worth the effort. A dear friend of mine called the other day and said, "Brother John, every time I hear you speak, you make me realize how good God is and how good He has been to me." If this book does that, it was worth it all!

The Laughter

*N*ow let me prepare you by saying that some people say, "He's not all here!" when they refer to me. If you heard me talk, you might think the same thing. My speech is slow, and my vocabulary is limited. I tell people, "I may not be all here, but I'm sure having a good time!" Due to various and somewhat difficult circumstances, my medical records list my illness as "asceptic" meningitis. Asceptic means that the exact kind of meningitis I had is not fully known. My financial resources were limited also, which I will later explain. God knows, and that's all that really matters! That also means that neither I nor anyone else can clearly explain all of the complications or implications of my illness.

All I can say is that I lost my memory of the past at some point in my illness. My memory now extends only back as far as October 1995, and it is very sketchy and limited even now about things that have happened since that time. Sometimes my short-term memory works better than other times. It depends on how I am feeling, along with the duration and intensity of my headaches. I still lose days and parts of days for some reason, but I've never lost the Lord, and He has never lost me!

A phrase I used often when I would see people from my church or pastors on my prayer list was, "I know you!" That didn't mean I remembered their names, unless My Donna had just been telling me who to expect. Maybe I had seen a picture from our church directory or been told something we had done before. I just somehow knew I knew them! Strangely and wonderfully, that was only true of those on my prayer list; and since all my church family was on my daily prayer list along with preachers I had known for years, that included a lot of people! It was like God had implanted them in my heart even though they were gone from my mind! I think that is so neat! God surely is good!

One day when the confusion and memory loss had reached its worst, I could not remember who I was or even who my wife and kids were. Everything was blank! That is when my dear wife, Donna, sat there and told me, "You are John, and I am Donna, and we are *married.* I indicated I did not understand the term "married" in my very, very limited ability to communicate. She then explained what *married* meant by saying, "That means you belong to me, and I belong to you!"

I said in broken words, "So, you are My Donna?"

She said, "Yes," and gave me my hug, smile, and kiss which has sustained me through so many trials. From that day to this, I call her "My Donna." I love her dearly, and she loves me a whole lot!

I look normal, or at least I think I look normal, whatever that is! My motor skills are somewhat limited, but not nearly as much as they were at first. Although I could get around if I watched myself carefully, especially when it came to steps, it took me nearly two years to learn to walk again with a certain degree of normality. I still have difficulty with steps. I can drive a car now even though I have trouble walking up steps. That's a scary thought! Once after I had driven to a church to preach, I stumbled going up the steps to the pulpit. I heard a woman in the front row say, "How can he drive when he can't even walk up steps?"

I turned and said, "I don't drive up steps!" I get on the sidewalk once in a while, but never up steps! I will have you know that I have now been driving over two years and had only one wreck. I hit a pole in a parking lot that I think shouldn't have been there in the first place!

My most difficult and lasting result of my illness is pain-- excruciating and debilitating headaches that can be very difficult to withstand even with proper medication. God did another one of the many good things for me when He had Dr. Bivens recommend Dr. Carl Covey as my pain specialist. God has used this Christian physician to help me deal with and work through my pain. I think my ability to keep going and traveling is due greatly to the Lord's using this man's wisdom and skill in my life.

Long battles with pain can be so discouraging and depressing! Believe me, I know! Yet, I have found the Lord is so good to always give His grace to help in those times! Many others have joined me over these years in praying for God to take the pain away. He has relieved it by making the episodes less frequent and the duration shorter most of the time, but He has not chosen to take it away. Some will no doubt charge me with a lack of faith and various other faults for not finding complete healing. I will deal with that later, but let me just focus on grace.

Although the prayer to be completely healed has not been answered in its entirety, God has answered one prayer every time I have prayed it: "God give me grace!" I am not going to get upset or mad at God for not answering some of my prayers the way that I want Him to when I get answers every day to many prayers, especially one of the greatest anyone could ask for: GRACE!

Never take for granted what a great thing grace is! The apostle Paul, who suffered in many ways including a painful condition in his body, referred to it as his "thorn in the flesh" in II Corinthians 12:7. God's answer to him was in the following verses, *"For this thing I besought the Lord thrice, that it might depart from me. And he said unto me, My grace is sufficient for thee: for my strength is made perfect in weakness. Most gladly therefore will I rather glory in my infirmities, that the power of Christ may rest upon me."* Paul was so happy with that answer. Instead of the healing that he stated, he would *glory* in his infirmities!

Wow! That's what grace can do! It can even make you happy that you have something painful if it results in God getting more glory and your having more power in your Christian life. I, for one, would rather have God's power with pain than no pain and no power! That very Greek word translated here as "glory" is also translated "joy" and "rejoice" elsewhere in the King James Bible (the text I will use throughout the book). Grace can turn pain into joy and hurt into happiness! I love to tell kids, "I'm a few fries short of a Happy Meal, but I'm happy!" I love the sound of laughter!

I consider myself a loving dad to my three sons, and yet there are times I tell them "No." A good heavenly Father can tell us, "No!" anytime He wants to and still be good! A good God knows what is best even if what is best seems wrong to us. A good God can know much more than I will ever know since He is an all-knowing and all-wise God. Why get mad at God? He's offering grace.

Getting mad at God will solve nothing and make everything worse! He is the only One that can help you and give you grace in your trials. Just think about it this way...if you are saved and know Jesus Christ as your personal Saviour, one day God is going to give you a new body that will never hurt again! He will put you in a place called heaven to live with Him and all the wonderful things that exist in that heavenly city described by John in the book of Revelation.

He will do away with the devil and anything evil and bad once and for all. Satan is the cause of all the heartaches, pain, and suffering, and God is going to punish him for it, too! It takes a good God to think up something that wonderful!

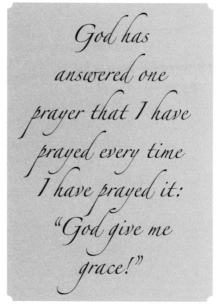

God has answered one prayer that I have prayed every time I have prayed it: "God give me grace!"

To make it possible for us to go to that place, God Himself had to become a man in the person of Jesus Christ. He died on the cross after enduring the worst suffering we can conceive. His suffering that day on the cross was not just bodily suffering but spiritual suffering. He took all our sins and our sorrows on that cross so we could be forgiven, be saved, and live with Him forever! IF YOU AND I HAD TO SUFFER EVERY DAY FOR 100 YEARS, THAT WOULD STILL BE SMALL COMPARED TO LIVING FOREVER IN HEAVEN!

Don't get mad at God! It's all going to turn out alright for the people who are saved. Now if you are not saved, please turn to the back of the book right now and learn how to simply and quickly get that settled. Don't wait and put it off! The Lord loves you and wants to help you now, but you have to choose.

You might ask, "How can He be good and make a place like hell as well as a place like heaven?" Please understand this: God is not only good any more than He is *only* love. Read the first part of Romans 11:22, *"Behold therefore the goodness and severity of God."* God can be severe at times with those who reject Him. To reject an eternal love demands an eternal punishment!

One time an atheist heard my testimony on tape, and he got saved. Here is what he said: "How could I have turned down such a good God all these years?" How can you turn down such a good God that makes you such a good offer? It took a good God to send His only Son, Jesus, to die for us! It took a good Savior to die such a death for us! I am not saying Christians never have problems. We do! I was a pastor when I was struck down with my illness. The difference is this: we have hope, help, and God with us through our trials!

If you would like to turn to the back of the book on page 144 at any time to learn more about this salvation, feel free to do so!

Fun along the Way

Sometimes people say I'm crazy. Usually they say it laughingly, but some may really think it is so! This usually comes in response to my many adventures or misadventures in the past seven years. I get so tickled even telling them, although I didn't always laugh when they first happened! Especially the many scooter wrecks I had! Let me relate my favorite scooter wreck, and then I will sprinkle a few more in for you as we go along.

I was going down the road on my Honda 80 scooter. Wide open is 35 mph, and I drove wide open to keep from getting run over by the traffic. I always wore my helmet except only once when I misplaced it for a day! I had my visor up since it was hot with my protective eye gear on. Suddenly I had to yawn, and so I did. Don't ever do that! While my mouth was wide open, a crazy bug mistook it for a cave or something and decided to go in and have a look around! He went down my throat so far that I couldn't get him up or down no matter how hard I tried.

I started to panic, which is not uncommon for me, and drove for the side of the road. The side of the road was the scene of most of my spectacular scooter wrecks. I knew the ditches well on that stretch of highway. I even named one ditch the Devil's Ditch! I

13

had spent considerable time in it in the five years I was limited to driving scooters. In my panicked state of mind, I turned off the road only to find some trucker had left the greater part of one of his tires there for a souvenir. I didn't see it in time to swerve. I thought, "Oh no, that's all I need! A wreck at this time. Which one is going to kill me first, the wreck or the bug?"

When I hit the tire, it caught in the wheel cover, and my front wheel stopped immediately, which is not good at that speed! I flew over the handle bars a considerable distance, landing face down in the ditch. I hit so hard on my stomach that it knocked the wind out of me. Guess what? The bug came flying out, too! Praise the Lord! God did a Heimlich maneuver on me to get that bug out! I did ask Him if He would please not be quite so rough the next time! The truth is that a wreck was all I needed at that time! God knew it, but I just didn't see it until it was over. Many times I wonder what I would have done on the side of the road if I hadn't had that wreck. How would I have gotten that bug out that was choking me? God is good!

My scooters are not the only source of fun for me over these past seven years. My Donna and I have had our share of good ol' fun times with silly things happening. At first my eyesight was so distorted that I would miss her lips when I tried to kiss her. I always kissed till I found them, though! That got to be so much fun that I missed on purpose at times. It was just fun finding them!

With this in mind, let me relate to you something her childhood church did for us after my illness. We were married in that church in 1973, or so My Donna says. I've seen the paper to prove it! One time I really got in trouble when I teased her by asking, "Are we really married, or are you after my money?" Once her home church learned of my memory loss of our marriage, they secretly arranged a "repeat" for us. I wasn't in on it at first. I thought I was just going up to her little town of Morrisonville, Illinois, to

When they announced our wedding, I got excited! They brought back the pastor, Dale and Shirley Montgomery, who married us twenty-three years before and his wife Shirley. They even brought in the best man, Brother Mike, and his wife, Cathy, who was the maid of honor. They met at our wedding and later got married. Many others were there, too!

What a lovely, gracious thing for a church to do for us! They are great folks! See, I have been married to My Donna twice. Now, remember, at that time I did not have very good aim at her lips! She was a little worried about that matter prior to the second wedding. So she said to me, "John, I don't want you missing in front of everybody. So you hold still when he says, 'You may kiss the bride', and I will do the kissing."

I said, "Nothing doing! Pucker up! I'll do my own kissing!" So I did, and I think I did pretty good.

I usually would get in the "neighborhood" of her lips, but I remember one time I missed the "neighborhood" and was in another "state"! She was laughing so hard, I finally gave up and hugged her. You ever try kissing somebody laughing their head off at you and trying to hold it in so they won't embarrass you? Try it sometime!

"You sure smell good! What do you have on?" The above question was posed to me when I walked out of our bathroom. My Donna wanted to know what cologne I had just put on since I smelled so good, or at least different than normal. I answered, "Nothing! I didn't put nothing on." She couldn't believe that. So she entered the bathroom and saw beside my sink the can of room deodorant sitting where I normally had the hair spray sitting. I smelled like a pine tree! Ladies, don't change to that for hair spray because it may smell good, but it just doesn't hold worth anything! I think life could be much more fun for us all if we would just look for it; I love looking for it!

I have had to learn so many things that seem childish to grown-ups. I think that is why kids seem to love me. I think so much like them. I am not sure why dogs seem to love me also! Well, anyhow, I had to learn to never say, "I don't like that!" in regard to people's food at their table.

It is all right to say that at a restaurant, but not at the house! I learned what I call a "Mommy" thing at one house. I know My Donna must have felt so embarrassed teaching her 45-year-old husband manners like a kid, but she was patient. (Except when she kicked me!)

Here's how it happened: I had embarrassed my dear Donna the second time by mumbling something about the food our dear hostess served us. I think I would have gotten by with it if she had only had one thing I didn't like, but not two things! That second item could have been used to write the second verse of "Set My Soul Afire, Lord" with these words: "Set My Tongue Afire, Lord!" Well, about the time I blurted out something and drank half my tea glass empty, My Donna kicked me in the leg good and hard while nicely smiling at the dear lady and saying, "He's not used to that yet." I call that kind of kick a "Mommy" thing! I have learned that I like a kick better than a stomp! Those stomps on the toes and feet hurt worse!

My dear Donna is such a sweet, kind person. She has been so patient with my childishness, even though it has caused her some hurt. Some of my foolish fears have led to arguments. Yes, I said *arguments*--arguments brought on by my fears and misunderstandings. God has given her more grace in dealing with me and my problems than most people will ever know. We are not a perfect couple, but we are perfectly in love!

Can you imagine having to teach your husband everything again? Some of you wives think you would love that, don't you? Believe me, it is not all that easy. My dear Donna had to teach me everything, including the intimacies of marriage. We have both done a lot of crying and holding each other over these past seven years.

I love for her to hold me and hug me when I am hurting emotionally or physically. Sitting up on the end of our couch, she has gone to sleep while holding my head in her lap when I was hurting so badly.

You are going to love me for telling this! I am going to help cheer up the world with this one study I did! You are going to say that the book was worth the price just for this one thing!

I have learned the wonderful power of touch in these past seven years! For instance, I could tell that the nurses and doctors who seemed to care the most would simply touch me on the arm, shoulder, etc... I could sense their caring by that touch. Others seemed to do what was needed with never a touch. I can't explain it, but there is healing in a touch. My Donna learned how much that meant to me, and I remember just brief moments of waking up while I was in and out of consciousness finding My Donna there touching me and saying kind words. I only recall a few words, but the gentle touch will forever be remembered.

I think her hugs and touches have done more for me than any medicine! Did I tell you what I learned reading a source on kissing one day? I've got to tell you this. You are going to love me for telling this! I am going to help cheer up the world with this one study I did! You are going to say that the book was worth the price just for this one thing! The power of the kiss!

Normal preachers wouldn't use a story like this, but with me, people just say, "That's Brother John!" I read in a real scientific research that when two people who love each other kiss, it elevates a chemical in their brain called dopamine. Scientists attached probes and did tests after these couples kissed, as well as when parents kissed children. When two people in love (That's My Donna and me!) kiss (That's what My Donna and I do!), it elevates this chemical called dopamine which helps trigger seratonin in the brain.

Stay with me! I am fixin' to get to the good part! Seratonin and dopamine are the "feel good" chemicals in your brain. The release of these makes you feel good! You catching on? When people are diagnosed as being "clinically depressed," they are usually given medication to elevate levels of one or both of these chemicals. When you kiss, you get it free! Boy howdy, wasn't that good! So when I am feeling a little depressed, I say to My Donna, "Honey, I am sure feeling down. I need my medicine!" She reaches over with a big smile and gives me my "medicine"- Sugar! I like the "lipilated" kind better than the "granulated" kind! I think that is why people get "dopey" when they kiss. It's that surge of dopamine! (In case you don't know me, I made that last statement up myself!) Now aren't you glad you bought this book? Just show this to your mate, and life will feel better whether it is or not. Notice I said you're mate as in married people. Teens, you don't need seratonin or dopamine! You're "dopey" enough as it is! Get a hug or kiss from Mom or Dad.

From the Silly to the Sublime

I want to talk about the cross of Christ now. You may be thinking, "How can he go from kissing to Calvary?" I am just being me. I go from laughing to crying so easily, maybe too easily. I can go from a simple thing like hugging and kissing to reminding others of the suffering on the cross. Kids are like that, and so that is probably why I am, too. One of my favorite junior speakers at camp is Evangelist Ed Dunlop. He is awesome with kids. In his services, I see kids slide so easily from laughter to brokenness and back again. I think that is the mentality of a child, which is really what I have. Yet, I think God uses it.

I speak to all different kinds of hurting people as I travel now. I always tell people, "Jesus understands and knows exactly how you feel when you are hurting. He knows how it feels!" One time I didn't take time to explain my main reason for making that statement. Here is my main reason based on Isaiah 53:3-4, *"He is despised and rejected of men; a man of sorrows, and acquainted with grief:....Surely he hath borne our griefs, and carried our sorrows: yet we did esteem him stricken, smitten of God, and afflicted."*

This is plainly telling us He bore not only our sins but our sorrows on that cross! According to this, Jesus carried every sorrow on Himself that day that I have ever carried since that day.

Since I believe He bore all my sins that day and they were all future, I can believe He somehow bore all my future sorrows that same day. Do I understand how He could suffer for all my future sins? No, but I believe it because God said He did. I don't have to understand everything I believe. I don't understand atomic fusion, but I believe it.

A dear lady challenged my statement "He knows how you feel when you hurt" by saying this: "How can Jesus know what it feels like to have your face beaten in by a drunken husband, then have him drag you by the hair of the head down a flight of steps and throw you in the street like a piece of trash for the garbage man? He is a man not a woman! He couldn't know the terror and pain I was feeling!"

My heart was touched and broken by what she said. So I said, "Please sit down with me a minute when the others leave the auditorium." We sat down on the pew, and I took her to Isaiah 53 and the above verses. I asked her, "Are you saved? Do you know Christ personally as your Saviour?"

She answered, "Yes."

I asked, "Do you believe Jesus bore all your sins on the cross when He died?"

She said, "Yes!" without hesitation.

I then said, "Were all your sins future?"

"Yes," she said. "What about your sorrows? Were they future, too?"

I saw a tear come to her cheek as she saw what I was saying. "Yes. He does know! He does know! He knows exactly what I felt that night because He felt it on the cross!"

Both of us were in tears now, and she squeezed my hand and quickly placed her cheek next to mine. I felt her tears. She quietly said, "Thank you, Brother John. You have answered a question for me I have had in the back of my mind for years. He knows. I feel so much better really knowing He knows!"

"Yes. He does know! He does know! He knows exactly what I felt that night because He felt it on the cross!"

I think many times, I had to become ill to really grasp that truth, although I probably knew it before my illness. I don't think you have to get sick to understand that truth, but I think it means more to others knowing how precious that truth has been to me.

23

Embrace the Cross

*J*esus not only bore "His" cross to Calvary, He called on us all to bear our own cross -- Luke 9:23: *"And he said to them all, If any man will come after me, let him deny himself, and take up his cross daily, and follow me."* Notice He said, *his* cross, not *a* cross or *the* cross, but *his* cross. That is saying that each of us has our own cross to bear. There will be suffering at times in the Christian life for all who follow Him. Peter reminds us that following in the steps of Christ is also a calling to suffer -- I Peter 2:21: *"For even hereunto were ye called: because Christ also suffered for us, leaving us an example, that ye should follow his steps:"*

Putting these principles together gets me so excited as I realize that any suffering that may arise in my life not directly related to my sin or sins is part of the cross Christ has for me. What's so exciting about that, you ask? It gives meaning to suffering. Sufferings of the body due to pain, illness, or mistreatment by others were part of Christ's cross. That gives meaning to our suffering. We never have to worry that any of those things were just wasted, meaningless, or worthless!

We have a name for them -- our cross. It is the same kind Jesus bore. We are even assured that it enables us to be partakers in the very suffering of Christ! I Peter 4:13: *"But rejoice, inasmuch as ye are partakers of Christ's sufferings."* Was Christ's suffering in vain or meaningless? No! Neither is our suffering. On that cross and on the way to the cross, God was at work in Christ. He is at work in us also. God allowed everything that happened to Christ that day on the cross. Everything!

God was completely in charge of everything the angry, wicked mob did that day. No, He didn't make them do it or even tell them to do it. However, He did know they would do it, and He allowed it. He allowed them to mock, torture, beat, whip, spit upon, and curse His only Son. Was it wasted? No. A thousand times no! The greatest good that could ever happen resulted from that cross!

Now if you are suffering because of bodily pain or sickness as I am, just remember that suffering is part of your cross. If you have been abused in some form or rejected by those you love so dearly, take heart; it is called your cross. If you bear it willingly as Christ did by saying, *"not my will but thine be done,"* you will be rewarded greatly, even as Christ was rewarded. If not, you will miss the blessing. Embrace the cross!

I find it so hard to convey to you how beneficial this principle has been in helping me with the terrible suffering in my body and the rejection I get at times from others. When I realize it is part of my very own cross, I know that the following truths apply to my suffering:

1. A Purpose - Just like the suffering of Christ has purpose, so does yours and mine. God had a great purpose in mind when He allowed the sufferings of Christ. My sufferings have purposes in God's mind even though it may not seem so at first. It didn't seem that way to the disciples of Christ that night and day of the dying of Christ! Any time sickness or circumstances force themselves into your life, rest assured God has a purpose in letting those be part of your cross.

2. A Plan - God had a plan for His Son and the world that included the suffering of the cross. It didn't just happen! He allowed it all to fulfill His plan. That plan was so complicated nobody, including those He taught so long, could understand or even accept it for a long time. The cross was in the plan just like it is in ours. When God withheld His protection to allow His Son to suffer so much that day and even forsook Him in those sin-darkened hours on the cross, it wasn't because He was unloving or unable to do something. He was doing something! He was saving us. It may seem as though it is for nothing while you suffer, but He is doing something. We just can't see it from down here.

God has a PURPOSE & PLAN for everything.

Let me illustrate what I think the difference is. If I get drunk and drive my scooter down the road into a tree (Believe me, I don't have to be drunk to run into a tree!), I will suffer for it. That pain isn't my cross. That's my chastisement! Now, on the other hand, if a drunk driver runs into my car, and I suffer with pain the rest of my life, that is my cross. Do you understand the difference? Things that just happen to us are part of God's plan with some purpose and meaning behind it that we cannot see right now.

My dear, dear Donna tells me of the time she had a miscarriage of our first child. She spoke of the emotional pain she bore. She then added it was worth it because I led a new daddy to the Lord in the waiting room that night. What made her pain bearable? It was knowing that there was meaning and a grand purpose behind it all. We lost a child at just the very night and even hour that this dad would be present so I could lead him to Jesus. It was part of the plan!

My meningitis was part of the plan for my life. God has a

great purpose behind my pain and suffering! His plan is unfolding every time I travel to another church and tell how good the Lord is. That is so exciting! A part of my very own cross is meningitis. I accept it willingly. God wasn't sitting idly by while Christ was laying down His life, nor was He doing so while I was lying in the hospital. He was doing some of His greatest work!

Many times when my pain seems unbearable, I remind the Lord that I know He knows how much I am hurting right now. Letting Him know that I am glad He has a plan gives me comfort. He has hurt with me and even now hurts with me. I think I will probably go to heaven one day when I am having one of those terrible headaches. The Lord will look down from heaven and say, "John, you and I have hurt long enough! Just come on home!" He is *touched* with the feelings of our infirmities according to Hebrews 4:15. In other words, He knows how we feel! In the meantime, I know He will always give me the grace to bear it. He will give it to you also! God is so good to be a God that can be touched by us poor humans!

Other people are touched when I hurt also. I have seen My Donna in tears so many times when I am crying. I love my sons and my church family because they care so much. Although I no longer attend the church where I pastored at the time of my illness, I love those people dearly. I will always love them although I know I have at times caused them some heartache through my trials and weaknesses. We cried a lot together in those early days of my illness. My Donna spared me much embarrassment by helping me recall names. I could honestly say to them, "I remember you," but My Donna had to help me remember their names and how I knew them. Sometimes she would say, "Now, Brother or Sister So-and-So is coming. Here is how you know them and love them!" She would never tell me anything bad that had happened between us. If difficulties arose, she was careful to share only what she felt was helpful; she tried so carefully to say only what was necessary and always tell me the good about them all. Those people at Cleburne County Baptist

"He is between the Rock and a hard place."

Church will never know how much I love them! All of them!

It's not all that bad to lose your memory. For instance, I have forgotten all the bad as well as all the good. I know some people whose past haunts them. They would give money to lose their memory! Mine did cost me a lot of money in hospital bills, etc., but it was worth every penny of it!

You have heard the old saying, "He's between a rock and a hard place." Well, I don't mind the saying if you change just one word and one letter. Say it this way: "He's between the Rock and a hard place!" Just put me next to Jesus, and I won't care how hard the place is.

Everybody Needs Church Home

1 am privileged to have two pastors at the time of this writing. The pastor of my home church, Gospel Light Baptist Church in Hot Springs, Arkansas, is Dr. Eric Capaci. He is a fireball for the Lord and has one of the biggest hearts for souls, saints, and sinners you will ever find. I sure love him and the dear people of this church and feel so loved by them. My pastor and my church love me so much. They have showered me with gifts, but more importantly, with love and understanding. Dear reader, if you do not have a "home" church or one to which you belong and are truly a part of, you need to do that now! I make no apology for being an Independent Baptist that truly believes, preaches, and loves the Bible! Whatever your choice, just make sure the Word of God is truly honored along with a compassionate outreach to the lost and hurting in your community! God describes it as "speaking the truth in love"!

My other pastor is my oldest son, Mark. Mark pastors our mission church, which is called Gospel Light Baptist Church of the Rose Bud/Heber Springs area. Mark loves the Lord and loves souls. He can say more in ten minutes than I can in one hour! We have grown to an average of 140 in just ten short months, even though we are located on a three-lane highway in between two small towns of only 6,000 and 429 people! We have baptized nearly forty people in a horse trough. As we get the money to buy a building, we are converting into a church with an actual baptistry! Somebody asked me the secret of such growth. I think I saw it one day when I stopped by Mark's church office to pray with him. As we knelt to pray, he broke into tears and brokenness for lost souls and the sheep under his care that were hurting. I knew then one of the great reasons for God's hand on him and our church!

My pastors love hurting people that are down and out. We have wonderful bus ministries which pick up the kids and adults from poverty-stricken and down-trodden areas of our cities and counties -- people that cannot add to us financially, but just need a hand up out of their hurting. We bring them in and love them. This always leads to further help such as clothes and groceries for these families, but we love them, and God blesses that love with beautiful lives. My pastor, Dr. Eric Capaci, has driven a bus to pick up such kids himself for twenty years! He loves them, and they love him!

Dr. Capaci and Mark do not compromise the truth, but they speak with love. They seek with patience to help the hurting person find the help they need. Hurting people need patience. When you find them, many times hurting people are lashing out at everybody including God. You must be patient with them as they work through some of their problems! Job certainly lashed out at God and friends! Sometimes crying with them does more good than talking with them!

I am glad both my pastors emphasize how important it is to be filled with the Spirit and led by the Spirit to help the hurting. After all, He is called the Comforter in John 16:7: *"Nevertheless I tell you the truth; It is expedient for you that I go away: for if I go not away, the Comforter will not come unto you; but if I depart, I will send him unto you."* Even though He is the Comforter, I have found He needs human hands to touch hurting people and human lips to say, "I love you."

I love my friends! I have so many, especially my preacher friends. Before Dr. Capaci became my pastor, he once challenged the pastors of our great state of Arkansas to help me finish paying for my last scooter (I still have it!) and buy me another four-wheeler. Yes, I wrecked four-wheelers, too! Those churches banded together and sent me hundreds of dollars. I will never forget that! Nor can I forget my dear friend Brother Eddie Flowers challenging the preachers and people at his fellowship meeting to give us the money to get a van for me to ride in right after my illness. Brother Eddie and his people have a heart of gold for hurting people!

I won't forget my dear old preacher friend Brother Lester MacKinnon having me just stand and give a few minutes of testimony when I could barely speak and having his people come by to give us a love offering! He didn't know that their generosity would make it possible for us to pay off one of our most difficult medical payments. God knew! Lester showed me pictures of me preaching a youth revival in his church when I was in high school. I had black hair at one time and a bunch of it, too! Many of his dear people have known me since high school. They call me by a nickname that no one else ever uses but dear Brother Lester and his people. It's none of your business!

My Donna and I had tried to prepare for medical emergencies by being involved in a Christian sharing program that helped with medical emergencies. It is not an insurance, but works similarly. It is more limited than insurance in the event of something as catastrophic as this was. Although it did help us so much at the onset of my illness, it was unable to keep up with ongoing medical needs. There was some mismanagement on the part of some of their executives that led to a lot of people getting stuck with bills and being hurt. We were one of many. We finally gave up and went elsewhere, but it has left us without some coverages. God has provided so wonderfully!

That's where my dear Mother would sit and tell me childhood stories. She is with the Lord now, and I sure miss her! While there, I was invited to give my testimony in two other churches I had preached at while a student at East High School. One was Victory Baptist Church where Brother Austin Cook is the pastor. Dr. Howard Robinson is a member of Brother Cook's church, the first pastor My Donna and I ever had after we were first married. He is one of the sweetest men of God you will ever meet! He did my mom's funeral because I just couldn't preach it myself. I'll cherish that memory and his words to my grave.

Many other friends have helped us. Brother Jerry Eggers is still pastoring the other church in the little town of Abingdon, Virginia, which is right outside of Bristol. He also wanted me to come, since he has people there, like himself, that could remember me in my college and high school days. When they poured their generosity on us, his dear people didn't know that day that My Donna and I had been crushed by an unexpected medical emergency that wasn't covered under our medical plan. God knew! My dear neighbor Brother Arlton dropped by to see me and left a fifty dollar bill. And Earl, a great neighbor who doesn't even attend our church, visited with me and left a gift behind. My dear dentist, Dr. Rob, not only helped save my teeth (I'll have a good story about that later!) but gave us a kind gift to help us through a very dark time he knew nothing about when he shared it. God knew! I could go on! Brother Payton gave me my first car after I learned to drive again. The men of my church built a ramp for me to walk up and took care of dozens of things I couldn't do around the house.

I told the Lord one day that it would sure be a good story if He would just drop me down about $15,000 to pay all these medical costs and catch up on things that were piling up on us. Surely, I reminded Him - as if He needed reminding - He had some millionaires that wouldn't miss that much! He never sent that, but I tell you what He did do! He sent me all those heavenly messengers I mentioned above and that I will mention later to

34

take care of every need. We always had the money to pay the monthly payments just when we had to have them. Even though we had to pay several hundred dollars a month for several years, it was always there. IF YOU ASK ME, THAT'S A PRETTY GOOD STORY LIKE IT IS! As a matter of fact, I think the Lord's version is better than mine. He is so good! (I've done got teary-eyed!)

We were left with huge bills, and the cost of medications will go on forever. Yet, God has provided with so much. I am not poor. He takes good care of His children. We have even bought us a nice double-wide mobile home since that time. I was fifty years old before I ever lived in a home with two bathrooms, but I do now! They are handy, too!

You know who is my best friend of all? Sure you do! Jesus! Please don't think I am a Pentecostal or a charismatic because I think we need to be filled with the Holy Spirit. Jesus had to be filled before He faced the hunger and temptations of Satan in the wilderness according to Luke 4:1. The Scriptures teach this for all Christians. (Ephesians 3:19, 5:18) I do not speak in tongues, and you don't have to either to be filled with the Spirit! We all need the power of God, especially to face suffering and affliction. Look what the Apostle Paul told his "preacher boy" Timothy in II Timothy 1:8: *"Be not thou therefore ashamed of the testimony of our Lord, nor of me his prisoner: but be thou partaker of the afflictions of the gospel according to the power of God."* He needed the power of God for those afflictions, and so do we. When you are filled with Him, you are filled with the Comforter. What an awesome thought! Why not pray, "God, fill me with your Spirit as I partake of these afflictions?" Spirit-filled Christians handle problems better than anyone else I know.

I was both humbled and honored one Sunday night a few months ago by my pastor and home church in Hot Springs. Dr. Capaci felt the Lord wanted him to take under his wing this stammering, old, broken-down preacher. I have placed in my calendar beside that night these words: "One of the greatest nights of my life!" I would sound boastful to tell all that happened, but I will mention one thing. My pastor has had many great preachers of days gone by to preach for him and help him build one of the greatest churches in Arkansas! He honored them by having their pictures placed in the church's Hall of Faith. I did not deserve to be placed there with such great men, but he did it anyhow. It has humbled me knowing that I was there for only one reason -- suffering. All the other men can preach or did preach great messages and were used of God to build great works for God's glory. Not me! Those are to be placed in high esteem because they preached to the multitudes and could draw hundreds or even thousands to Christ. I am sure all of them had great trials, but me? I am just there because God gave me the grace to keep loving, trusting, and serving Him as the weakest of all the preachers. I do not say that in mock humility; and if you ever heard me speak, you would agree. I tell people, "I'm not a very good preacher, but I am a pretty good pleader."

There is another reason I am there! It's called love. These people just love me so much that it doesn't matter to them I can't speak very well! For all of the others, their works done in the Spirit were being honored. For me, it was simply grace, not works, that brought the honor. Even though our church knows I am a "few bricks shy of a full load," they love me. Isn't love a wonderful thing? Love blinded them to all my disabilities. Love does exalt the lowly, just like God's love for us! I want that kind of love for others!

That night My Donna and I wept while Sonya and the choir wept and sang a song written and composed by one of our dearest ladies, Sonya Chittum. I think Sonya is the greatest female vocalist in Fundamentalism. She wrote a song based on one of my frequent sayings when I give my testimony, "God is always good, and God is always right!" You can order a copy of it on our new tape or CD if you like. I cried when I heard a song that reminded people that God is always good and right simply based

God is always good, and God is always right.

on how He is helping me through my suffering! Her other CD that features songs she wrote such as "Faithfulness," "Only God Sees," and "One Touched Life" is awesome, too, for hurting people. Good music has helped me so much!

I wish poor old Job could have had the friends I've had and the wife I have! Tears come to my eyes as I recall these things. I have been so loved! One evangelist friend of mine, Dr. Ken Hovind, even offered us several hundred dollars out of his own pocket if I wanted to pursue another medical treatment facility. Thank you, Brother Ken!

When I was brought home from the hospital one time, my dog came and laid his head in my lap when they opened the car door on my side. He looked up at me with those pitiful eyes like he was saying, "I have missed you, and I love you." Laugh if you want to, but I remember saying, "Even my dog loves me!"

If you are not surrounded by the love of others like I am, please do two things:

1. Realize, if you are saved, the Lord loves you as much as He loves me or even His own dear beloved Son according to Romans 8:35-39! You are never unloved even if you do not have the support of those around you like I do. You also have this promise in God's Word, (Psalms 27:10) "When my father and my mother forsake me, then the LORD will take me up."

2. This second request is so important! Show and shower somebody who is hurting with the kind of love you wish you had or would have in your suffering. Be that kind of loving person you would want others to be toward you.

If you will honestly and sincerely do these two things, get ready, because God is getting ready to send you a lot of love!

My Preacher Stories

1 'm behind you one percent!" Now being behind a preacher friend only one percent isn't much when you are in a battle! I was writing a dear friend of mine, Dr. Vineyard, a letter of support because he was taking an unpopular stand on an issue and taking a lot of heat for it. I kept a copy of the letter because I wanted to be sure of what I said to him and others during the difficulty.

I meant to say, "I am behind you one hundred percent in this matter!" What happened is this. When I was typing this letter, My Donna was nowhere to be found. I could not remember what to place after the number *100*. I tried @, #, $, &, and %, but none of them looked right to me. So I decided I would just print out "one hundred percent," but I left out the word "hundred." So it read I was only behind him *one percent* . He is so kind, he didn't even tell me, but his associates got a good laugh over the phone as I confessed to him my error. I told them to tell Dr. Vineyard, "I'm up to two percent now and climbing!"

Once, a pastor took me to see this beautiful glass structure where they grow great and exotic plants and some birds. I saw for the first time real live "Love Birds"! There are birds called that! I am not making this up! If you see them you will know why, because they perch right next to each other with their little heads and necks laying on the other. I loved it! I couldn't wait to tell My Donna!

I wanted to go up to the top to see more, but we didn't see an elevator. I insisted, although he wasn't too much for the idea. You see, I had to go up on my hands and knees to keep from falling. I do that when I am not sure about the steps. It looks a little weird; but I figure that if I am already down, I can't fall down. Nobody was coming; so we started up. Here came a couple down. This crazy thought hit my mind! Actually a bunch of crazy thoughts live in my mind, but this one was really good! When the people got close, I said loudly to the pastor behind me, "Please don't hit me; I'm trying!"

Well, they did stop and gave us a funny look! They looked as if to say, "Are you alright? Are you serious?" I laughed and said I was teasing. I then heard the pastor mumble something about "killing me" when he gets me out of the place! I decided to take my time looking at the plants while he re-gathered his senses. Preachers, please don't be afraid to take me in public. We will have a good time, or at least I will!

I like the one where I signed my letter to a pastor this way: "Your fiend." I left out the letter *r*. Did you know that there is only one letter's difference between being a friend and a fiend? My spell check on my computer didn't catch it since it is an actual word. If I ever send you a letter and something weird comes out, let me know! I might use it one day.

I once wrote a dear Christian saying that I missed being able to *sin* like I used to! I meant to say *sing* like I used to sing. I heard a tape on which I sang before my illness. I'm really not that much worse now, but I am just more embarrassed by it! I am trying to work on my singing and my embarrassment, but not making much progress with one of them. I'll let you guess which one it is!

The Tears

J hope you have already shared a little in my laughter,
but I am sure you know there were a lot of tears also.
Tears because of physical pain do not reveal nearly as much hurt
as those from emotional, mental, and psychological pains! I have
cried myself to sleep more because of heartaches than headaches.
I remember many nights of my family showing me pictures of my
past and talking of some of the good things we had done together.
Many times, I would cry myself to sleep and ask God, "Why
did I have to lose so much? Why couldn't I at least remember
my children growing up, my wedding and honeymoon, or other
wonderful events?"

Do not get me wrong. I loved those memory building
times, and they do not bother me nearly as much now. Sometimes
I am just overwhelmed at the loss of so many precious things dads
and husbands can treasure, but I usually love to try to imagine
what things were like back then.

I wrestled with fears of many different kinds, some real and
some imaginary. The one constant fear and dread was the next
headache and the thought that I will have to live with this the rest
of my life! It may well be that I have to live with pain the rest of

my life, but the headaches I used to have two or three times a day are now only coming two or three times a week with less intense ones in between them. Praise God!

Once in a while, I think the headaches decide to bunch all up for a really big one, but God always gives grace. Some are more severe than others, but with space between them, I can prepare my mind and spirit by clinging tightly to the unseen hand of God! Sometimes the headaches are so bad that they cause leg cramps that hurt so bad that My Donna rubs them until they let up. Many nights she has rubbed them for long periods of time while I wait for the spasms to quit. God is so good to give me someone so kind and tenderhearted!

Why would God say, "No," when I asked for relief of my pain? Why would He not want to stop that for me, His child? Now, keep in mind that I couldn't read at the time these thoughts were going through my mind. I was virtually house-bound and nearly bed-ridden. What big thoughts for me these were! I was trying to learn all I could about the God I knew. I was listening to Scripture on tape three hours a day, most days. I was asking some questions to others, especially My Donna. I came to this conclusion: a child-like faith was all that God required of me! I loved the idea of child-like because I might be able to handle that. If it was adult-like faith, I was a goner! Adult thinking, much less adult faith was out of my reach. My thoughts and really much of my reasoning were so childish.

I began to look at little children, and my youngest son, Luke, was only ten-years-old at that time. He loved me so much and taught me so much by sitting and talking to me. He believed me and everything I said simply because he was a child. I loved it when little children would come see me. We thought so much alike. We were both about as dumb as each other! You see, losing your memory hinders a strong faith. Much of a person's strong faith is based on their memory of Scripture. The children's faith was helping me renew my faith in the simplest form. I decided I would believe that everything God said was right. He is my Father. Since I

> *Believing He is always good gave me assurance that He is good even when we are hurting.*

am the child, I know I cannot understand or know everything, but I can believe everything! I was convinced that since the Bible is God's Word, I would believe everything the Bible said. Have you come to that simple child-like faith in the Bible?

My Donna and others shared with me the research that I had done in the Bible before my illness. This research had led me to use the King James Version. I kept very extensive notes on all my studies, for which I am very grateful. My research since my illness has also led me to the same conclusion! I preach and teach from the Old King James, and I have absolute confidence that I have the Word of God. When the thought hit me that the Bible is the very words of God, I was thrilled! You can argue about translations if you want to, but I am happy where I stand!

Now, this sounds silly I know, but I figured that since I am not smart, how could I possibly question something the Bible said? I think that is a good way to look at the Bible even if you have a good mind! Why should any of us think we are smart enough to question the Bible? Once I arrived at this position, it was easy to arrive at this all-important conclusion: God is always good, and God is always right! Believing He is always good gave me assurance that He is good even when we are hurting. Believing He is always right assured me that He knows and does what is best (including my pain), even when I cannot understand the issues involved. Issues like pain, suffering, and heartaches take on a new meaning from this perspective. It must be faith and especially child-like faith for this to happen.

I realized either God is good just like the Bible says or He is not at all. It was all or nothing, not partly true. I chose to believe He is good and, since He is an unchanging God, good all the time! (*Psalm 25:8: "Good and upright is the LORD: therefore will he teach sinners in the way." Psalm 118:1: "O give thanks unto the LORD; for he is good: because his mercy endureth for ever."*) He was good the day I got meningitis. He didn't stop being good the day I got sick. It isn't fair to God to just call Him good when everything is going well. He is good all the time! Notice that Psalm 25:8 also says God is upright. God is always right. The truth of God always being right about everything stood out in my mind. These two truths gave me an ever-increasing peace and actual joy! (*Deuteronomy 32:4: "He is the Rock, his work is perfect: for all his ways are judgment: a God of truth and without iniquity, just and right is he.*)

Believing He is always right assured me that He knows and does what is best.

You might be wondering, as many do, "How did you know you were saved if you couldn't remember the day you got saved?" I cannot explain it to you completely, but let me do my best. I think it is based on Romans 8:16: *"The Spirit itself beareth witness with our spirit, that we are the children of God."* The Holy Spirit lives inside of each of His children. I didn't have to have somebody tell me I knew God. I somehow knew I knew Him! I just needed someone to tell me how I knew Him. The basics. My Donna and others did that. I could give you my testimony today because I have it memorized, but I don't remember the events personally. At one point, a physician told me, after hearing my mumbling over a period of time, that the only word he could make out was the Word *God!* It was like I forgot everybody and everything but God. That's awesome! I keep telling you God is good!

It was helpful to me to read handwritten accounts of my testimony in one of my old Bibles and a typewritten account in a book I had written years before my illness. One Sunday after my illness, I gave a testimony in my church to encourage people to put into print their own testimony, in case they ever lost their memory like I did. I also said it would be good for the pastor to have at their funeral. Two people told me they came to the Lord because when they started to write theirs, they realized they were really not sure if they were saved. Praise the Lord, they were saved after that day! Why not have a testimony service at your church? Preach from the great testimonies in the Bible and have people from all different walks of life give theirs that day. It can be a great day!

Being around kids a great deal began helping my childlike faith also. I would hear a child say, "That isn't right," only to find later when they were told the bigger picture, they realized that the adult was right. It just did not seem right at first because their knowledge was limited. As strange as it may seem, things like that excited my faith! There are a lot of things like that down here. Things that, to us humans, look wrong, but we cannot see the whole issue like God does. God does not have to explain such things in order for them to be right, just like a parent does not have to explain things to a child in order for them to be right. Things can be right without our understanding or approval. That was a great thought to my feeble mind!

Why does not the Bible answer all my questions? Has that thought ever crossed your mind? I used to sit and wonder why God did not just make part of His Bible a "question-answer" book. Remember, I was closed up in the house alone for many hours over the course of several weeks and was very limited for more than two years. When I say alone, I want you to know that my family was always available since My Donna taught in our Christian school, which was located on the same campgrounds where we lived. I insisted that she go back to teaching because I was smothering her at this point. She needed to get out of the house for her sake. A friend who pointed this out hurt my feelings at first, but the Bible says in Proverbs 27:6, *"Faithful are the wounds of a friend;"* Now, I am thankful.

I have come to this conclusion: the Bible is about God, Who He is, how He works, what He desires, and what His ways are. God knows that the better we understand Him, the fewer questions we are going to have. Knowing <u>Who</u> is more important than knowing <u>why</u>! I love to tell people a wonderful truth which came to me after studying the powerful book of Job. God did something better than answer all of Job's questions; He took the questions away! Job did not have any more questions by the end of the book. At the beginning of the book, questions were mostly what Job had. How did God take the questions away? Did He answer his "whys"? No! He just told Job Who was in charge and showed him some of His greatness and power.

Job's biggest problem was with God, not the devil. The charismatics would have had Job rebuking the devil. Do you realize that God is the only one who mentions the devil in the book of Job? Job came through his darkest night just talking to, dealing with, and wrestling with God. If we get our view of God in the right perspective, God will take care of the devil! I am not saying there is no place to mention or deal with the devil. No! I am just saying that we need to deal with God first. Get to know God better. You see, Job had a little problem with God being in control. God was doing all these things without asking him or allowing Job to change His mind about things! Job 23:13 says, *"But he is in one mind, and who can turn him? and what his soul desireth, even that he doeth."* Job is saying that when God makes up His mind, one cannot change His mind. Well, he is only partly right. If you read the rest of the Bible, God gives examples of His servants seemingly changing His mind. However, we must accept the fact that God is going to do what His "soul desireth." Job accepted this. One day I hope to write a little booklet on some of the things I have learned from the book of Job. We all like for God to be in charge, except when He seems to bother us!

God, Did You Get Tickled at That, Too?

I want to speak with absolute reverence to God. I never want to demean or belittle any aspect of God in any way. You may think asking God if He was tickled at something that happened to you is irreverent, but I think He enjoys life with me. I had a string of little things happen that tickled me. Really, I have them happen all the time. Let me just give a few early ones that I like.

Once, I got in the shower to bathe. I reached for the shampoo to wash my hair, put the shampoo on, and rubbed; but no bubbles appeared. I thought that was odd, but I just figured it must have lost some of its power and poured extra on the next time. I rubbed and rubbed again with no success. I just rinsed my hair the best I could and got out of the tub. I told My Donna, and she investigated. She found out I had used her body oil instead of shampoo. She had to scrub my head twice to get all the oil out! I "shined" for a couple days after that, too!

I have thanked the Lord for helping me miss my mouth with my toothbrush; I have done that often in the past few years

when I had something on the brush besides toothpaste. At first, I missed my mouth because my eye and hand coordination was messed up. It is still not normal. At this particular time, I was experimenting with men's styling hair cream because I had a few accidents of spraying my eyes with hairspray. I often sprayed my eyes because I could not tell which way the spray was coming out. I thought the cream would solve that problem since there was nothing to spray. However, I left it sitting on the bathroom counter close to the toothpaste. You guessed it. I grabbed it instead of toothpaste. Thankfully, because I have a bad aim, I got very little in my mouth. Most of it landed on my upper lip! It tastes terrible!

I cannot really remember after which incident I looked up to the Lord and said, "Lord, did you get tickled at that, also?" Why would I say or think that? My opinion is that God is looking down from heaven with love and laughter as I would if it were my children. I love my children. I like to play with them, tease them, and laugh with them when funny things happen around them. I like to laugh when funny things happen to me, and I think the Lord has a good time, too! Why don't you try to think about the Lord like that? You see, I think He cries and hurts when we cry and hurt. Isaiah 63:9: *"In all their affliction he was afflicted, and the angel of his presence saved them: in his love and in his pity he redeemed them; and he bare them, and carried them all the days of old."*

I think He laughs with us, too. Look for fun things in your life. They are there if you just look.

Books from Broken Vessels

ooks written by the brokenhearted have a certain "ring" about them. They are the great enduring books of time. They are called classics. The authors have a certain endurance about them. It seems their brokenness has been used of the Lord to put something in their writings that touches us all, or at least all of us who have been broken. These men and women have things jump off their pages into our hearts. They have a way of bringing a tear with a truth that stays after the tears are gone. Let me share a few books the Lord has used to touch me during these past few years. Let me hasten to say that I do not agree with every writer on everything. I may have some disagreements, but we have something in common: we are fellow sufferers. These books have helped me and may help you also.

Charles Haddon Spurgeon is said to have more books in print than any other minister in the twentieth century. His books are mostly made up of his sermons that have stood the test of time. He was so open and honest in his messages about his battles with depression, sadness, and melancholy! Most preachers today would be terrified at the thought of sharing their struggles with depression. Think of this preacher who preached to some six thousand people three times on the Lord's day. He would get so depressed that he had to cancel preaching appointments because he could not overcome his times of depression! He was successful in every sense of the word, as far as ministry is concerned. His books were the most popular of his day; his church was the largest in the English-speaking world. He had a wife who adored him and whom he adored. He had two fine sons, one of which became the pastor of his church after his death. Why would he be depressed?

I think this shows us that anyone can be spiritual and so-called "successful" yet still face discouragement. Listen to the words of Spurgeon in one of his messages: "With heights of joy in serving my Master, I am happily familiar. But into the very depths of despair -- such an inward sinking as I cannot describe. I have likewise sunk. Yet I do know that my Redeemer lives, that the battle is sure, that the victory is safe." He talked of his dark times. We can "mine" some precious gems from messages he gave during the times of his great trials. Some biographers have put together historically the time periods in which he was under stress with the great battles of the "Downgrade Controversy," physical illnesses, and other tragic events. Those times produced some wonderful sermons.

Listen to this powerful quote: "I am subject of depressions of spirit so fearful that I hope none of you ever get to such extremes of wretchedness as I go to. But I always get back again by this: I know I trust Christ...Because He lives, I shall live also, and I spring to my legs again and fight with my depressions of spirit and my downcast soul and the victory through it." Note the words like "wretchedness" and the phrase "fight with my depressions." This is real; it is a real battle we face, as well. I carry his sermons and books on joy and overcoming depression. They are still helping people over one hundred years later!

The book of another broken vessel comes from the pen of Hannah Whital Smith, who penned the classic *The Christian's Secret of a Happy Life*. If we knew just half the heartaches she lived with, we would marvel that she could find happiness, much less write a book on it! The nightmare of Hannah's life began the day some Christians involved in her husband ministry caught him with another woman. You see, her husband was an up-and-coming evangelist in the late 1800s. He was preaching to crowds of two or three thousand in England and in America. Hannah was devastated by this event. Although her husband denied that the actual act of adultery had taken place, he became very bitter at her, God, and the church. She remained married to him although he became a traveling salesman, who claimed to be an agnostic and had a reputation for being immoral on his trips. In other words, she endured a horrible marriage.

Besides the disappointments of her marriage, Hannah's heart was to be broken further by the deaths of four children. One of those was a sad and tragic event. To hurt her even more, she had a daughter reject her own faith and follow the example of her father away from God. This daughter went so far as to marry a famous atheist of her day. Hannah also had bouts of depression and poor health. Physicians now say that depression itself can bring upon, or at least complicate, matters of poor health. Understanding this, it should not surprise us that Spurgeon suffered more greatly at times with his gout than at other times; nor should we be surprised to hear that poor Hannah struggled with poor health at times in her own life!

Her book on happiness was actually started as a series of articles for a Christian publication while her husband was in the ministry. She was later motivated to put it into book form because of a remark she heard an unbeliever say: "You Christians seem so unhappy and miserable. Like somebody with a headache, you want to get rid of the ache but keep the head!" This moved her to challenge both herself and her readers to live a happy life in front of the world. Are you challenged to live a happy life so that unbelievers will want what you have?

She compiled her articles into book form because of her Christian periodical's wide acceptance, even by the late D.L. Moody. She said she had truly a secret that enabled

> *"You Christians seem so unhappy and miserable. Like somebody with a headache, you want to get rid of the ache but keep the head!"*

her and others to have happiness, even if their worlds were falling apart with disappointments and heartaches. Her book is still selling by the thousands over a hundred years later!

I also love her later book called *The God of All Comfort*. My favorite chapter in that book is called "The Goodness of God." During some of her darkest hours, she wrote, "Somehow it did not seem worthwhile to go on living..." Do not miss what she wrote later in her life: "Trouble and sorrow, therefore, are not our curse, but one of our most cherished rights... Why should we allow ourselves to be so needlessly unhappy with thinking that our trouble is one in which God has no part?" What an awesome thought! God has a part in our trouble.

Another great devotional writer who battled with illness, pain, and depression was Amy Carmichael. Amy has produced great books and poems. Most preachers who desire to read devotional classics have read or heard of Amy. Her book entitled *If* really touches my heart. Here are some excerpts before I give you a little sketch of her life.

If I do not feel more for the grieved
Saviour than for my worried self
When troublesome things occur,
Then I know nothing of Calvary love.

If in dealing with one who does not respond,
I weary of the strain and slip
From under the burden
Then I know nothing of Calvary love.

If I am perturbed by the reproach and
Misunderstanding that may
Follow action taken for the good
Of souls for whom I must give account:

If I cannot commit the matter
And go on in peace and in silence,
Remembering Gethsemane and the cross,
Then I know nothing of Calvary love.

If I cast up a confessed, repented, and
forsaken sin against another,
And allow my remembrance of that sin
To color my thinking and feed my suspicions,
Then I know nothing of Calvary love.

If souls can suffer alongside,
And I hardly know it,
Because the spirit of discernment is not in me,
Then I know nothing of Calvary love.

If my interest in the work of others is cool:
If I think in terms of my own special work:
If the burdens of others are not my burdens
too, and their joys mine,
Then I know nothing of Calvary love.

Many people close to Amy, although they knew she was a dear, dear saint, felt that she could, at times, show a little self-pity and impatience. They did not paint her as perfect but truly a godly, suffering saint. She was born in 1867 in Northern Ireland. She never married but felt strongly called to the mission field. In 1892, she was rejected by China Inland Mission for her frailty. Because of this, she went to Dohnavur, India, commissioned by the Church of England, where she served for fifty-six years. Some of her serious health problems started in 1894. God used her to start a great orphanage to rescue "temple" children forced into prostitution and horrible abuse. To this great outreach was added a hospital and other ministry outreaches. Her life was not without controversy. Disagreements with other Christians caused her to break ties with all mission societies. She was crippled by a fall in 1931. She became bedridden in 1935, and poor health made things very difficult. She was practically immobilized from 1948, until the end of her life in 1951. From her pen came some of the great encouraging words and books that have inspired me and others who have bad pain; pain that did more than just pay us a visit, pain that came to live with us longer than we may have wished. Much longer!

I love this beautiful image she showed of her love and burden for those dear suffering children: "There were days when the sky turned black for me because of what I heard and knew was true...Sometimes it was as if I saw the Lord Jesus Christ kneeling alone, as He knelt long ago under the olive trees...And the only thing that one who cared could do, was to go softly and kneel down beside Him, so that He would not be alone in His sorrow over the little children." I would cherish "black" days that would bring me to Gethsemane like that! God is so good!

Oh, to be like Christ is my plea to God! I once heard of a man who intended to create a lion out of a huge rock. He was asked how he thought he could make a lion out of that rock. The sculptor said, "I intend to chisel away everything that does not resemble a lion." Now getting "chiseled" and "hammered" on is no fun; but if it is for the purpose of making us more like Jesus, it is worth it! God uses pain and trials to chisel away self to make us like Himself.

Let me share just a few sayings about God's goodness and blessing that I have read and that have blessed me.

"Be assured that if God waits longer than you wish, it is only to make the blessing all the more precious."
- Andrew Murray

"O God, I have tasted thy goodness, and it has both satisfied me and made me thirsty for more."
- A. W. Tozer

"Our God is so wonderfully good and lovely and blessed in every way that the mere fact of belonging to Him is enough for an untellable fullness of joy!"
- Hannah Whital Smith

"God's people are never so exalted as when they are brought low, never so enriched as when they are emptied, never so advanced as when they are set back by adversity, never so near the crown as when under the cross. One of the sweetest enjoyments of heaven will be to review our own experiences under this law of compensations, and to see how often affliction worked out for us the exceeding of His glory."
- T.L. Cuyler

When Pilgrim in Bunyan's book saw the Valley of Darkness and Discouragement, he said, "I see not but that my road to heaven lieth through this very valley." May God help us see this also!

When Pain Comes to Stay

1 n most lives, pain visits us in some form or another. It may be pain through guilt or other emotional trials that are either inflicted by self or others. To some, physical pain enters their lives to visit a while. Usually pain takes leave with simple measures like taking aspirin or other over-the-counter pain relievers. Some can cause pain to leave through other physical exercises combined with a positive attitude or perhaps some form of therapy. For those, pain quietly exits just as it quietly came. Be thankful, dear chosen ones; lift your voice in thanksgiving to the God of mercy for this!

To some, pain stays a little longer with each visit; to others, it stops by more often, such as those with chronic illnesses or conditions such as headaches, back problems, and a whole host of chronic ailments too many to list. (I will not try to list them all for fear someone reading this may feel slighted that I may not have felt their condition worthy of a list of painful conditions. I will just mention two I know personally, and hope you get the idea I am trying to get across.)

When pain comes knocking on your door, a few people have the strength and ability to ignore his visit and go on with life.

Others can send him away with medication quickly and easily. But to some of us, pain knocks so loudly we cannot ignore him as much as we try. He pounds so hard that we cannot just dismiss him with an easy remedy. Into a few of our lives, he knocks the door down and comes in against our pleas and prayers. He is a most uninvited guest, an intruder into our lives.

When pain comes to stay or to live in your life, everything is different. He is so rude. He invades every party and breaks up every occasion with his presence. He is a robber of everything he can carry off and everything he can get by with. He is so hard to stop! You can shoot him with pain-killing drugs such as codeine, morphine, and more; yet he laughs at those remedies and laughs in your face as you cry. He is such a sinister, hideous being that taunts you with such words as, "I'll never leave! I have you now, and I will never let you go! The next time will be even worse, and it will always get worse! You will never find relief!" To some reading this book, that seems like a bizarre description of pain, maybe even a contortion or exaggeration; but for far too many of us, pain is more real than the description of a hideous monster.

He is such a messy intruder. He makes a mess of your emotions. He scatters them all around. He makes you cry, scream, and often feel isolated. Even though you may be surrounded by love everywhere, pain makes you think you are singled out for his presence. He does something so awful that you feel you must surely deserve this thing called pain. Depression and loneliness can invade your life when there are really no good reasons for them.

I cannot explain it, but nobody in this world was surrounded by more love than myself. My dear Donna, family, and church literally showered me with love, yet I sometimes felt swallowed up with loneliness and depression. The presence of pain can do that. If somebody reading this has no support like that, please know that some of your fellow sufferers will reach out with a love and sympathy you have never known. I will risk being bombarded by hurting people by insisting to the publisher that my ministry address be listed in this book. With God's help, I will respond somehow to each one.

In the weeks and months just after my illness, painful headaches visited me several times a day. This pain, at times, took my very breath away, making me gasp for air; at times I thought it was unbearable. Three and four visits a day were not uncommon. The fury of those visits brought me such despair that I begged God to take me home to end this nightmare! I do not know why I did not contemplate suicide as many do during this stage, but I did want to die. I do not think it was because I was stronger than others or had greater faith. I sometimes think it was because my mental capacity for such things was more limited. Violence of any form would have been a terrifying thought to me. However, I did get angry at God a few times for not answering my prayer to go home. I say that to my shame. Should I be ashamed of that? I really do not know.

I remember one week I counted the hours and minutes that would pass before the next round of pain would come again. I would think: "I can make it that many minutes or hours, and maybe it will get longer between visits." Although I could not really comprehend time, I could keep up with the clock between intervals of my pain. I remember crying tears of joy and saying to God, "Thank you, thank you so much for that extra five minutes of less pain!" That may sound little to you, but five minutes longer between episodes gave me hope. Hope is a very precious thing to sufferers. Minutes turned into an hour; eventually that turned into days. Oh, how I praised God for a pain-free day! Some of you are still counting minutes. I have occasional days that I suffer two or more attacks; those days serve to remind me of where I came from. Dear sufferer, I love you. Try to make it a few more minutes. Do not try to hold on to days right yet, just minutes. You can do it!

Even though some of us cannot make pain go away, we can try to ignore him all we can. I say "all we can" because it is sometimes impossible to ignore him altogether. We believers in the power of God know that He could order pain to leave any time

Our view of how good God is, is not based on our seeing how bad we are; but seeing God's grace, love, goodness, and mercy behind every gift. Humility is not the same as self-condemnation, but God-exaltation. When I think of how good God is, I am humbled. I want to be like Joshua and Caleb and not just see that my blessings are "good," but "exceeding good!" Those who walk by faith see it. Continue to join me in the journey into the next chapter.

and forever, if He wanted. Will we get mad at Him for not doing so, or will we believe He only leaves pain there because He has some greater good by doing so? Pain's presence in my life has brought some good things to my life along with the bad - not just good, but wonderful things. I am sure that pain and his bestower, Satan, are saddened to know I actually believe it is best for me if pain stays in my life. Knowing that I actually thank God at times for pain's presence must surely aggravate Satan, but I do. I truly am stronger spiritually when Satan's visits drive me to my knees, making me feel my need of God more keenly than ever! God is so good!

I read that great missionary David Brainerd said these words: "Oh, for holiness! Oh, for more of God in my soul! Oh, this pleasing pain! It makes my soul press after God!" I also believe those words; although I admit, they are hard to say sometimes!

The Strange Work of God

I have come to love an unusual phrase in Isaiah 28:21: *"For the LORD shall rise up as in mount Perazim, he shall be wroth as in the valley of Gibeon, that he may do his work, his strange work; and bring to pass his act, his strange act."* This text is a blessing to me and can be to you. God is warning the nation of His people Israel that judgment, severe judgment, is coming on them for their sins. It is similar to the harsh judgment that He used on the wicked nations of Perazim and Gibeon.

We think it strange when God deals with His children seemingly harshly. In this text, God told Isaiah to give His children a special understanding about the judgment. God gave them a word picture of how He would deal with them, like a farmer deals with his different crops when he threshes them at harvest time. Each grain is dealt with differently, based on how it is made and what it can withstand in threshing. For instance, he states the cart wheel is not turned upon the cummin; cummin is a delicate, tender grain that would be destroyed if the wheel were used on it, like it is on some of the wheat grains.

In other words, God will only use what is necessary and no more to "break" us or "crush" us so that we can be used. You see, the threshing of a grain is not to destroy it but to make it usable and edible. Until that hard outer surface is broken, it is of no use. God knows we are that way, too! We must have our hard outer shell broken to be usable. It seems strange to us when God has to break or crush His children. We think sometimes, "What a strange way God has of dealing with that saint." However, we can rest assured He is not being too rough. He knows whether to use the "wheel" or the "staff" to break us. Just as a farmer knows what instrument to use on his precious life-giving grain, our heavenly Husbandman knows what each of His dear children needs.

He told Isaiah another comforting truth in God's dealing with us. In verse 28, He assures us He will know exactly how long to thresh us as well. Note: *"...he will not ever be threshing it."* He knows how long it will take and that it will not be a minute more; although I must be first to admit that I think it is too long at times. Two questions David often asked were, "Why?" and "How long?" Sometimes it does seem too long, but it never is. Peter also knew we would think God's dealing with children in hard times would seem strange. I Peter 4:12 says, *"Beloved, think it not strange concerning the fiery trial which is to try you, as though some strange thing happened unto you."* It really should not appear strange to us that God would use fiery trials to make us into His likeness, but it does at times to us all.

I also love this final thought Isaiah gives us in verse 29: *"This also cometh forth from the LORD of hosts, which is wonderful in counsel, and excellent in working."* Even though it may appear strange, we know it is "wonderful" how God does things and "excellent" beyond our wildest imaginations. It is so wonderful when we see life flow from our brokenness! It is so exciting to see good things come from broken hearts crushed in the threshing process. I pray, "Break me, O Lord!" Sometimes I add these words, even though I know He does not need them: "Be sure to use the right instrument, and quit as soon as you can!" God is too good to hurt us more than we need.

By Appointment Only

ometimes when I speak, teens and children come and ask me to sign their Bibles. I am humbled by this gesture of respect, but I would never ask for that privilege. I am amazed at times at some of the names of great preachers who have signed their Bibles before me. Nevertheless, when I do sign them, I write, "Brother John - Job 23:14." Why Job 23:14? Why has that verse sort of become what some call a "life verse" for me? I may change it some day, but I will explain why it is my life's verse for now.

At the time Job made this statement in this glorious chapter in the Bible, all the terrible things have happened and are still happening. With all of the death of all the children, the rejection of wife and friends, and the loss of every earthly possession, he says, *"For he performeth the thing that is appointed for me: and many such things are with him."* Think of what he is saying! He is saying these things are part of God's appointments in my life! They are by divine appointment! He is accepting and acknowledging these things without getting mad at God, although he does not understand it!

Here is a wonderful and beautiful thought also found in that verse that will bless you. The word *performeth* that Job used is also defined in *Strong's Concordance* as "make good." It describes how God will restore or pay again to us things we may lose. What verse does that remind you of in the New Testament? Romans 8:28 says, *"And we know that all things work together for good to them that love God, to them who are the called according to his purpose."* Job had a glimpse of a wonderful New Testament truth, which Paul saw thousands of years later: God was performing things for good. The main thing that I want us to see is that Job looks at this whole "thing" as appointed by God!

God has an appointment calendar for each of us. I carry an appointment calendar and put in it certain events for the year. It includes happy things I love, like birthdays, anniversaries, revival meetings, speaking engagements, etc. It also includes some things I would like to avoid if I could, like doctor's appointments, dental appointments, or funeral services. If I had my way, I would fill it with the good things all the time. It does not work that way in life, and God's calendars for each of us have both things in them as well.

God's appointment calendar for John Bishop had scheduled "meningitis" for October 1995. He had everything arranged for me. I just did not know it. He had a doctor on duty that day, who was not my family doctor at the time; but he was God's wonderful choice for me. His name is Dr. Frank Bivens. He has become a great source of help to me and my dear family. Dr. Bivens, his nurses, secretaries, and staff have helped me through more than I could even describe. They have wept, prayed, and laughed with me through so many things. The meningitis was just the beginning for them!

They have helped me through some of my nightmarish headaches. They were there when My Donna helped me hobble into the office after severely herniating a disk in my back. They watched me cry when My Donna brought me in with a crushed finger while trying to do some work at our youth camp. They were there when I needed some help getting over panic attacks which the headaches brought on. I could go on; but caring people, like this, were part of God's plan. I hope every person has the privilege of having such good health care professionals. God had arranged by appointment for my doctor to be there that day I was brought in to the hospital.

More Than One Kind of Miracle

To some Christians, there is only one kind of miracle - when you have a miraculous healing from an illness! I think God has other miracles available for those with long-term illnesses and pains, besides miraculous healing! He also has miraculous help and miraculous hope! God has worked both of those miracles in my life. He has helped me through every trial and disability that has come my way! He has also given me hope, incredible hope for the future! I love Him dearly.

I am like the psalmist that said in Psalm 46:1, *"God is our refuge and strength, a very present help in trouble."* That is an awesome thought! God is very present in trouble to help us. He has helped me through so many things! Do not try to convince me that His help has not been miraculous! I think one of the greatest miracles that we often overlook is the miracle of Divine help in our times of trouble or crisis. Dear reader, He has helped you through some tough times. The fact that you made it this far should amaze you and many others! Do not get upset simply because He has not chosen to heal but gives you miraculous help instead.

Although some of the improvements to health are

nothing short of miraculous, He has not chosen the path of complete healing for me yet. He has helped me so much that I try not to complain about the health problems. Once, I was hopelessly lost in the huge Atlanta airport, trying to find my gate. I had gotten off the train in the wrong place. I was walking and crying at the same time, praying for God's help, when a young couple came up to me and offered to take me to my gate.

Read more about God's help. Psalm 63:7: *"Because thou hast been my help, therefore in the shadow of thy wings will I rejoice."* Psalm 108:12: *"Give us help from trouble: for vain is the help of man."* There are times when no person can give us the help we really need, but God comes through! Psalm 115:11: *"Ye that fear the LORD, trust in the LORD: he is their help and their shield."* Make God your help and shield by trusting and relying on Him! Psalm 121:2: *"My help cometh from the LORD, which made heaven and earth."* The God of this universe wants to help you today!

Another miraculous gift from God in our pain and suffering is the miraculous hope. God gives wonderful hope, hope that defies human understanding, hope in impossible situations. Read some of these exciting verses on hope; then I want to share an incredible story of hope that you will love! Psalm 31:24: *"Be of good courage, and he shall strengthen your heart, all ye that hope in the LORD."* Hope produces the strength to go on when we feel we can't! Psalm 33:18: *"Behold, the eye of the LORD is upon them that fear him, upon them that hope in his mercy."* If you want to catch God's eye, you can do it by hoping for His mercy. Because God is merciful, even "plenteous" in mercy, you can be assured of help and strength.

Here is an incredible, life-changing story of hope! A few years ago in a small rural community, Reverend Clyde Thacker was brutally murdered by two teenagers. He was shot in the head and killed instantly. This dear pastor, husband, and father was taken from this earth. His dear wife of many years was plunged into a world of awful pain.

The court system inflicted further pain through long trials and many trying circumstances. She wrote a beautiful, encouraging book entitled *Tea and Sympathy*. This book has been used of the Lord to help and encourage others who are going through various kinds of pain. Her subtitle is *A Compassionate Book To Help Those Who Are In Pain*" She also published a ladies' magazine entitled *Perfect Feet For Women* in which she speaks of hope: *"God has graciously given me so much hope since the murder of my husband. The Lord has shown me that, with His mighty hand and out-stretched arm, there is nothing that is impossible for Him to do. He has taught me that there is even hope in seemingly hopeless times....He has wonderfully blessed me, and I want to proclaim it by sharing these tremendous blessings with you!"* She made this statement regarding her book: *"It is written from my heart and steeped in love. I pray that every word loudly sings out the message of hope."*

God's Word has given us hope! Psalm 130:5 says, *"I wait for the LORD, my soul doth wait, and in his word do I hope."* Love and read His Word for hope in your future. If you are saved, your future is awesome! God will see you through! One of the very reasons God tells us all those Old Testament stories and Scriptures is to produce hope in us. Romans 15:4 says, *"For whatsoever things were written aforetime were written for our learning, that we through patience and comfort of the scriptures might have hope."* The story of Job gives us hope that God will be there through the worst possible situations. The story of Joseph encourages us to know that God is working behind the scenes to bring good out of the bad things that happen to us. The story of David teaches us that God is there in our greatest failures even when our sins have brought on our suffering. The many stories of the children of Israel give us hope that He never gives up on His children, even when He must punish them for doing wrong. I could go on, but please realize that one of God's own stated purposes for His Word is hope.

God turns a valley of trouble into a door of hope in Hosea 2:15: *"And I will give her vineyards from thence, and the valley of Achor (trouble) for a door of hope: and she shall sing there, as in her youth.*" God sometimes turns our troubles into blessings and brings hope out of our darkest valleys. If you are in a valley of trouble right now, any kind of trouble, ask God to show you the door of hope for a better tomorrow and a better future! Then walk through it! Sometimes we bring trouble on ourselves, like in the text in Hosea, but God still offers hope! He promised them a door of hope on the other side of their valley. He offers you that same door of hope. Have faith in God! Here is a beautiful nugget of truth somebody shared with me: "Faith sees the invisible, believes the incredible, and receives the impossible!"

"Faith sees the invisible, believes the incredible, and receives the impossible!"

How different is the wonderful testimony of hope of Mrs. Victoria Thacker than that of a lady interviewed on the one-year anniversary of the terrorist attack on America whose husband died on that awful day of September 11. I was watching some anniversary news specials one evening when they interviewed her. It was so sad. She used phrases like, "I will never be happy again." "The pain just gets worse instead of better." And other phrases of utter hopelessness without any hope of heaven or the Lord. Brother Thacker's death at the hand of two teenagers, who shot him in the head at point- blank range with a large caliber handgun, was just as horrific. The difference is the Lord and the miraculous hope He gives us in times of great tragedy or sorrow.

Where Is That Man That Loves Me?

We have a church youth camp that My Donna and I started in 1975. We still live on the campgrounds in a nice mobile home. When the kids arrive in the summer, I am so happy and thrilled to see them. I try to look for kids who need a little extra help or seem to be slower than other kids. I sort of take them under my wing when they come. I befriend them a little extra. One such boy certainly needed extra attention. I sat with him during the evening service, so he would not be quite as homesick.

After the service, I went to the house for some much-needed rest, only to be awakened by My Donna. She said, "A little boy is crying for you. He couldn't remember your name, but he knew you had gray hair. He said, 'Where is that man that loves me?' We knew it was you." I went to the little fellow and comforted him his first night from home. That was one of the greatest compliments I could be paid by anyone! "Where is that man that loves me?" It was because I talked to him and sat with him in a service to assure him he would be all right. It was nothing big, just little things.

I wonder how many people would feel we loved them by simply showing a little extra kindness and thoughtfulness. I may not be able to do many things that others can do; but I can love folks, especially those who are hurting. So can you!

Think about How Good God Is

1 want everyone who reads this book to think of how good God is. I often pray before a church meeting, "God, please let everyone leave saying, 'God is so good!' not saying, 'John is good.'" My desire for this book is to cause every person who reads it to think how good God is, not how good I am. Anything good about me, you, or anybody else comes from God, not ourselves. Remember when David invited others to see how good God was in Psalm 34:8? *"O taste and see that the Lord is good..."* If you read the heading above this chapter in most study Bibles, you find it was not written while David was on the throne as the great King David, king of the greatest army in the world. No, it was written while he was running for his life and living in caves to keep from being killed by Saul. He experienced God's goodness even then.

Some people only sing of God's goodness when they reign, but David sang about God's goodness even when he was ruined. His whole life was in a wreck because of the jealousy and envy of one man, but God was still good to him. When some dear Christians built a nice home for Corrie ten Boom in California, someone said to her, "Corrie, God has sure been good to give you this beautiful home." She replied, "God was good when I was in Ravensbruck (the awful concentration camp where she and her sister suffered so greatly), too!" If Corrie could see God's goodness in that awful German concentration camp, surely we can see it in our situations. David could see it in a cave. Can you not see it in your car, house, or even in your valley?

I have failed if all you can see is what I have been able to do and not what God is able to do. According to the Bible, our peace depends on our thoughts. Listen to these verses from Scripture. Romans 8:6: *"For to be carnally minded is death; but to be spiritually minded is life and peace."* Isaiah 26:3: *"Thou wilt keep him in perfect peace, whose mind is stayed on thee: because he trusteth in thee."* We must direct our thoughts toward God. I got a wonderful thought in a book one day, but I cannot remember the exact wording. The idea was that it is not my job to think about myself; my job is to think about God, and His job is to think about me! Quit thinking about yourself all the time.

The more that we think about ourselves, the more depressed we become. The more we think about God, the more peace we have. He said He would give peace to those whose mind is "stayed" on Him. You have to stay with it. Your mind will wander. Make it come back and stay on the Lord. I often tell people that the difference between their mind and mine is this: your mind wanders; mine leaves town! When your mind is tempted to leave town, get it back where it belongs.

So many dear, hurting people miss peace because they have their mind on worldly or carnal things instead of on spiritual things like *"...to be spiritually minded is life and peace."* When you are thinking about spiritual things, you just have more joy and peace. When Paul wrote the letter to the Philippians, he told them in chapter 4 verse 4, *"Rejoice in the Lord alway: and again I say, rejoice."* He also told them about the *"peace of God, which passeth all understanding..."* While he was on the subjects of joy and peace, He gave some final instructions. Philippians 4:8: *"Finally, brethren, whatsoever things are true, whatsoever things are honest, whatsoever things are just, whatsoever things are pure, whatsoever things are lovely, whatsoever things are of good report; if there be any virtue, and if there be any praise, think on these things."*

God is saying if we want joy and peace, we must be careful what we think about! Many hurting, depressed people whom I meet make some serious mistakes that lead to further depression. One mistake is closing themselves up in their houses or rooms with a television set. Most of what is on television will not encourage you when you are hurting. Worldly or sinful things will actually rob you of joy. Keeping your mind on spiritual things would help you much more. Do not trade even a good television show for time that could be spent reading God's Word or good Christian literature. Limit your amount of intake of television and spend more time reading, listening, or hearing good Godly books on tape, especially the Bible. When you spend ten minutes reading the Bible and ten hours watching television, you are going to have a difficult time enjoying God's wonderful peace and joy. I listened to the Bible on tape three hours a day when I could not read it for myself. How uplifting that was!

Another mistake hurting and depressed people make is listening to worldly music, which only leads to more depression. The music of this world mostly features what people lose. God's music features what we have gained in Him! Good, Godly music goes along with the Scripture, telling us to be spiritually minded and dwell on true things. Most of the world's music is not true or honest; it does not tell how things really are or how they can be made right. The answers found in the world's music are not right. Godly music gives real answers to real problems. God's answers are faith, love, hope, etc; not alcohol, sex, or running away. Some of the world's music is not pure and will not lead to pure thoughts, thus robbing us of His peace.

I cannot tell you the number of times I have gone to see some dear, hurting soul only to find him "isolated" up in the house with his worldly music spewing forth its un-Christlike message! In those types of places, there is something missing that you see and feel

I love to watch how God turns our pain into power. He also turns man's mistakes into God's miracles! He turns our hurts into helps for others. Every week I hear of people who have been hurt that begin ministries of help to other hurting people. Ministries to the suicidal have been started by those who have loved ones who committed suicide. I have seen how a dear lady, whose daughter was raped by a pedophile, started a network that finds pedophiles for the police. Great things can be accomplished when we get our eyes off our pain and focus on others.

when in the home of some dear, hurting soul that has a tape or CD playing good Christian music. That is one reason I produced tapes and CD's with uplifting messages and music sung by various Christian friends that encouraged me most during the early stages of my illness. Godly music can help so much.

I am excited about heaven, also! That gives me a wonderful hope. Heaven is really what life is all about! We do not live for this life. I pray that the Lord will take me home quickly if the time comes that my mind leaves me completely. I do not want to be a burden to others once my time comes to go. Please remember, though, that I am still Brother John even if the mind goes. The soul and heart are still there. People who may lose their minds still have the Lord, even if they no longer know how to put their thoughts into words!

Right now, I have to lean more on Jesus and rest in Him. It is all right to be that dependent on Him. I truly feel like a helpless sheep, but that is okay with me. I feel every day and every hour, unless the Lord holds me tight, that I cannot make it in life. However, I am happy feeling that way! My illness has helped me in that way. God is so good to me!

It Helps to Laugh

I have had my share of slip-ups. Some are even too embarrassing to share; others have brought me nearly to tears because I laughed so hard. I remember getting a letter back from a pastor friend whom I had written. My closing for the letter was supposed to read, "Your slow friend, Bro. John." Instead I misspelled *friend* by one letter and signed, "Your slow fiend, Bro. John." There is a lot of difference between a friend and a fiend! He circled it and sent it back. He said he was glad I was at least a "slow" fiend and not a fast one, because fast ones cause more trouble!

Once while preaching, I could not remember the phrase "Throw in the towel." That phrase means you give up. So I was encouraging people not to give up; but after a pause, all I could think of was, "Don't throw in... the wash rag." At least I was in the same neighborhood! When I say to people, "Don't give up!" I know that is easier to say than to do. Sometimes it is hard not to give up.

I love to laugh when I tell my famous, or infamous, scooter wrecks. I had several wrecks during the nearly five years of riding. Once I was trying to outrun a roadrunner. I am talking about a real, live bird, not the one on cartoons. We actually have them here in Arkansas. He saw that I was getting the best of him; so he decided he would just start flying if he could not beat me on the ground. So he did. He flew right into my pathway and into my helmet with my shield up! Feathers were flying everywhere while I tried to blindly get off the highway and out of the way of some cars coming my way. Yes, I wrecked; but I learned a valuable lesson. The next time I start to pass a roadrunner, I make sure I go "Beep! Beep!" Maybe he will move over!

I had a dear preacher get up to preach after I had just finished my message in a conference and say these words: "Brother John, I want to thank you for helping me laugh. You will never know how much I needed to laugh tonight. God used you in my life to do just that!" I was blessed by those "thank-you" words. I do not want to be a comedian, or even a Christian comedian. I am a preacher, but I asked the Lord a few years ago if He would allow me to help people laugh. I guess the reason I want to do that is because I know how much laughter has helped me in my dark and difficult times.

I got on an airplane after a hectic delay. The flight attendant was assisting some grouchy passengers in front of me. Most of the passengers were still complaining about different things. One man in particular was taking it out on this attendant who was trying to assist him in finding more room for his oversized carry-on. I decided I would see if I could help her.

When this dear lady came to my row, she asked me what she could get me to drink. I told her a diet Pepsi and then said to her, "You had such a sweet spirit in handling that difficult situation. I just wanted you to know that you have been a blessing to a preacher today." You should have seen that smile! She could have swallowed a banana sideways with that smile! I love bringing smiles to peoples' faces. I hope I have yours.

Fear This

1 finally got to where I could drive a car after five years of Honda scooters. I went through four scooters in five years! I never hit cars when I wrecked, which was quite often; I just hit trees, ditches, fences, and an occasional stray animal. Considering all this, I survived pretty well. I dislocated a shoulder one time; this was my worst wreck. Most good scooters can handle about four wrecks before needing to be replaced. I found out the hard way!

When God delivered me from seizure medication and I passed an eye test for my driving license, I sure was shouting that day! Shortly thereafter, I resigned the church I had pastored for fifteen-and-a-half years to travel in evangelism. I knew that God was leading in that way. I was excited, and my dear church was so gracious to me. They had a "going away" fellowship for me. The young people got me this huge bumper sticker that said, "FEAR THIS!" I did not put it on my car, fearing somebody might think I wanted to drag race or something!

God has graciously protected me as I have traveled several miles preaching for Him and telling people how good the Lord is. I am reminded that I must overcome things that I fear. The devil has many "Fear This" signs that trip and hurt good Christians. We have to live by faith and not by fear! I have had to battle that since my illness.

We Christians should have a bumper sticker that says, "FEAR HIM!" The real issue in life is not "what" we fear, but "Who" we fear. Do we fear God or man? If we fear man, the Bible says it "bringeth a snare," but fearing God brings everything good that God has to give in His time and in His glory. It is not always here and now, but always eventually in eternity for His children!

Why

I say to congregations often that it is all right to ask God "Why?" if you are willing to receive the same answer Jesus got when He asked God "Why?" as He was hanging on the cross. God could have answered, "Why hast thou forsaken me?" with the same voice from heaven that He used at Jesus' baptism and at the Mount of Transfiguration. Both times, He spoke openly so that Jesus and others heard it. Yet, at the cross, He chose not to do so. God was silent that day. In a way, we might say that was the only unanswered prayer Jesus prayed when He asked God "Why?" Notice I said the words "in a way" in the sentence above. I used that phrase because we do not know if God answered in some other way or not. We just know He did not give an immediate, outward answer.

Can you accept God's silence when you ask "Why?" Job had to accept silence just like Christ did. God never told him "why." One dear Christian author took real comfort in saying that God never condemned Job for all his questions and even a few accusations verbally hurled toward God. I have to disagree to a certain extent; although He never "condemned" him, He did correct him. When God answered Job, He did not answer Job's questions. He started His answer with these words: Job 38:2, *"Who is this that darkeneth counsel by words without knowledge."* He also chides Job in chapter 40 verse 2, *"Shall he that contendeth with the Almighty instruct him? he that reproveth God, let him answer it."* I am glad God did not destroy Job for speaking out of turn or even for coming across like he knew better than God. We might all be dead! I think He would have taken me home a few times! Remember: God does not just overlook our words, even if His chastisement is not immediate. Job had to accept silence when he asked God "Why?" He settled with knowing Who. Can you be settled with "Who" instead of "Why"?

Notice just a few of David's "whys?" that God never answered. Psalm 10:1: *"Why standest thou afar off, O LORD? why hidest thou thyself in times of trouble?"* He accused God of standing by and doing nothing during his trouble and even hiding Himself. Psalm 42:9: *"I will say unto God my rock, Why hast thou forgotten me? why go I mourning because of the oppression of the enemy?"* Have you ever felt like God has forgotten you?

There were more <u>whys</u>, but God does not give any clear-cut answers. However, He did converse with David. Can you accept silence to your "whys?" Someone might say, "God spoke to David, but He does not speak to me!" You are wrong! He speaks to you through His Word! Did you know that no one with a Bible can say, "God never speaks to me!" Every time you read His Word, He speaks! As long as there is a Bible (Matthew 24:3: *"Heaven and earth shall pass away, but my words shall not pass away"*), we can never say God is silent to us. Please do not ever forget that; God is not silent, but He may be silent in regards to your "whys!"

I often quote the words found scrawled on the walls of a Nazi concentration camp barracks. As far as I know, nobody knows the author; but God has used mightily such faith under such conditions! *"I believe in the sun even when it is not shining. I believe in love, even in a world filled with hate. I believe in God, even when He is silent."*

I wonder how hard it was to keep on believing in God

when He did not answer their questions: "Why are you allowing this to happen to me?" "Why do I have to suffer like this?" "Why did you let them kill my family?" "Why..." a thousand other different endings could be added to a list of those housed in a place of such horrible death. My "whys" seem so little and insignificant compared to theirs. How about yours?

God does not have to say why He allows or does not allow certain things. I am comforted in knowing that even if He is just proving to the devil something, as in the case of Job, He still brings good to us all out of it! I am helped today because of Job; and so are you -- not because you have all the answers, but because you know that you can make it without all the answers. It is a goal of mine to somehow show the world that I do not just praise God when He is good to me materially and physically, but also during those times when I cannot understand Him at all.

Once in a while, God does give us a sneak peek at "why". I got one a while back that I want to share with you. My car broke down at a church where I was speaking. I got to the parking lot just barely before the car stopped. I mentioned it to the pastor. I think it was the pastor who had owned a car like mine. He knew what was wrong; he and a mechanic temporarily fixed mine. They showed me how to tape the "thing-a-ma-jig" to make it work until I could get the car home and to the shop to be fixed. Praise the Lord!

A couple of weeks later, I was driving to town and saw a neighbor of mine broken down on the side of the road. You guessed it! It was a car similar to mine, and it was the same "thing-a-ma-jig"! I fixed it. She was so grateful that she allowed her children to come to our church the next week. I had tried to get them before with no success. God used that incident to bring it to pass! I broke down so I could help somebody else who was broken down! Have you ever thought that your "break down" might just be so that you can help somebody else you will meet along the road of life who is broken down? Think about it.

I have learned that God has used fellow sufferers to teach me so many wonderful truths from His Word. I cannot explain it, but I have watched how God has given special insight to those who have learned from His Word during trials. I will not try to name all the books that have been so helpful to me, whose truths I, in turn, used to help others. The truths are not always the "earth-shaking" kind but just comforting little principles that you tuck away in the back of your mind. You bring them out when you are tempted to give up or when you meet somebody hurting like you.

"I believe in the sun, even when it is not shining. I believe in love, even in a world filled with hate. I believe in God, even when He is silent."

Here is one example: Dr. Henry R. Pike was so seriously injured while playing football that he lost the use of both legs for the rest of his life. He was only eighteen when that happened. That is quite a blow for a teenager! In his book *Suffering & Death: the Saint's Highest Calling,* he brings out many things he has learned in his life as a sufferer for and servant of the Lord. He has served the Lord for more than thirty years as a foreign missionary and in other ministries for our precious Lord. In his book, he is showing how the apostle Paul viewed his life and suffering: "Yet he had the spiritual discernment to interpret God into this whole experience. He was always *'a prisoner of Christ'*; never of Rome. His sufferings fired a new courage into the faint hearts of weaker missionaries and preachers..." I love that thought! He did not consider himself a prisoner of the state, but of the Lord, even though the state was the one causing his condition. God was in control, not the state! He figured he was there for a reason that the Lord knew, and he accepted that. That is a great principle to keep in mind.

Our Best Resort

S ometimes I hear people who have struggled with heart-breaking and difficult issues referring to an upcoming treatment or approach to their problems as their "last resort." Please do not ever say that. Never call anything a "last resort," or you may feel there is nothing beyond that point. There is always something beyond your next treatment or your newest round of help -- always! Listen to the words of David in Psalm 71:3: *"Be thou my strong habitation, whereunto I may continually resort: thou hast given commandment to save me; for thou art my rock and my fortress."* Make the Lord your first, last, and especially your continual resort! Never, ever, let medical or psychological treatments be referred to as your "last resort"! I am not saying to never use any of those approaches to your problems. Just never say that they are your last resort; meaning that if they fail, there is nothing else to help you. You always have God. If every treatment and medication you ever try fail, He never fails!

I have used medical treatments and some well-trained physicians to assist me in my life. God has used them and countless others in many difficult times. Here is the danger I have observed in the last seven years of dealing with hurting people:

> *Never look at anything as your last resort! You have God when everything else fails.*

the disappointments and depressions that follow those who refer to the next physician, treatment, or medication as their "last resort" can be horrendous if it does not work the way they expected. Some of the fault may lie in their expectations being unreal or faulty. Their hope may be based on somebody else's experience that may not be quite like theirs. One medication can work for one depressed person that may have no affect or even have an adverse affect on another person! Do not base your expectations on what happened to "so-and-so."

You always have God, even if nothing man has found has worked yet. Notice I said "yet" because so many things are being discovered every day! Some procedures used today give hope where there was no hope even months ago! Even if man never finds a cure or a remedy for your situation, you have God to Whom you can continually resort. He has something that no one yet has manufactured -- grace! You cannot put that in a bottle or write it on a prescription form and have it filled at the pharmacy, but I assure you that God will "fill" that prescription for you.

Something that has concerned me greatly in recent years is this: many people who have taken their lives by their own hands *(Please do not consider that as an option!)* have almost always done so after having tried a medication, medical treatment, or new approach that had supposedly failed. A couple of times I heard a comment made by a family member like this: "They had tried this treatment as a last resort and couldn't handle it when it failed." That is why I plead with people to "NEVER LOOK AT ANYTHING AS YOUR LAST RESORT!" You have God when everything else fails, even your repeated attempts to get help.

Sometimes people give up after battling problems that are brought into their lives by their own sinful behavior, thinking it can never get better. Remember that God forgave you the moment you repented and asked for forgiveness. The ongoing results can be very difficult. Think of poor David in the Bible. Think of the many things with which he had to live: his adultery with one of his most loyal soldier's wife and the murder of that man, his numbering the children of Israel in defiance of God's command (which resulted in the deaths of seventy thousand people), along with all the havoc his sons caused on his nation! I don't know anyone whose sins have caused such havoc to others, besides the so-called "monsters" who slaughtered others in wicked regimes like Hitler and others. No, David was not a mass murderer; but people did die because of his failures and wrongdoing. Yet, he kept throwing himself upon the mercies and goodness of God!

Make the Lord your first, last, and especially your continual resort!

Do not get me wrong; David did have his doubts! He wondered if God had cast him off forever or if He would ever let him see His face again. Psalms 13:1: *"How long wilt thou forget me, 0 LORD? for ever? how long wilt thou hide thy face from me?"* Now remember this is the same David that wrote Psalm 23:6: *"Surely goodness and mercy shall follow me all the days of my life: and I will dwell in the house of the LORD forever."* I hope I did not overlook any psalm that would contradict this next statement: although David still at times had depressions and doubts after Psalm 23, I could not find where he asked that question again. Now there are several psalms that do ask the exact or almost the exact same question to God, but

> ### "Keep a-Goin"
> by Frank L. Stanton
>
> *If you strike a thorn or rose,*
> *Keep a-goin!*
> *If it hails or if it snows,*
> *Keep a goin'!*
> *'Taint no use to sit an'whine*
> *When the fish ain't on your line;*
> *Bait you' hook an'keep a-tryin'*
> *Keep a-goin'!*
> *When the weather kills your crop,*
> *Keep a-goin'!*
> *Though 'tis work to reach the top,*
> *Keep a-goin'!*
> *S'pose you're out o'ev'ry dime,*
> *Gittin' broke ain't a crime;*
> *Tell the world you're feelin' prime*
> *Keep a-goin'!*
> *When it looks like all is up,*
> *Keep a-goin'!*
> *Drain the sweetness from the cup,*
> *Keep a goin'!*
> *See the wild birds on the wind,*
> *Hear the bells that sweetly ring,*
> *When you feel like singin', sing*
> *Keep a -goin'!*

those are all attributed to Asaph or other writers, not David. Will you let Psalm 23 be your turning point? Let that "surely" statement be yours, and go on for God!

Did David get mad and give up on life, thinking God would never help him? No! He threw himself on the mercies and goodness of God! He knew that a merciful God could forgive him and that a good God could help him through life. Please take ahold of that truth for your life if you feel you are suffering today due to your sin or even somebody else's sin or if you feel like you are to blame or partially to blame for another person's sorrow or even death. Please remember that others' sins can affect your life. You cannot control everything others do, and God has chosen not to control everything others do. We know God could; but in His wisdom, He has chosen not to do so. Therefore, leave it with Him and run to Him for refuge, as David did, when you are hurting! He is a refuge and a resort to those who hurt!

Reasons for Hope

One of my favorite New Testament books is the book of first Peter. It is written to hurting people -- people who have lost everything. He starts the epistle describing them as "strangers scattered" and describing the many places to which they have fled. People who flee for their lives usually do not get the luxury of taking all their heirlooms handed down from one generation to the other. They usually cannot just walk into the bank and withdraw their lives' savings on their way out of the country. No! They grab the clothes on their backs and stuff a few things in boxes and run as fast as they can. They leave it all behind. Everything they dreamed about is gone. Everything they worked for is gone in a few minutes. Yet Peter gives them hope!

Because of how they have helped me and others, I will just touch very briefly on some of the principles to help hurting people that Peter gave us. Let me start by giving you the challenge that God gives to hurting people found in I Peter 3:15: *"But sanctify the Lord God in your hearts: and be ready always to give an answer to every man that asketh you a reason of the hope that is in you with meekness and fear:..."* In essence, God is saying to hurting people that we should be ready to give people a reason for the hope that we have even in our pain. Are you ready to do that?

I love what I call the "sameness" of life. Each day has some of the "same ole, same ole" things that you just have to do as a part of daily living such as getting up, getting dressed, studying, and working, etc. My life of sameness consists of daily studying, weekly visitation and witnessing, and the daily routines. I love those days! I have found God doing some of His greatest acts in my life during my routine life. I refuse to just sit back looking for something "great" to happen and miss God's blessings in the daily routine. Many great things happen when we are just doing the same old things we have done for years. Unless I am very ill, I never miss our weekly church-wide visitation program. I may go weeks without anything special happening on visitation nights, but eventually "greatness" happens as I "happen" to be at the right place at the right time to reach out and help someone or be helped by someone! Everyday routines can often produce everlasting rewards when we give others reasons for our hope!

1. According to Peter, one reason for hope is *the resurrection of Jesus Christ!* He is alive and well. That should give us believers hope that He lives and we shall live also! Peter says in chapter 1 verse 3 that it produces in us a "lively hope." Are you a lively Christian? You should be! The resurrection of Christ gives us a firm foundation for our faith, according to I Peter 1:2. *"Who by him do believe in God, that raised him up from the dead, and gave him glory; that your faith and hope might be in God."*

When people ask me why I am so sure of the future, I quickly state, "Because of Jesus!" The resurrection proves that everything He said was true and that every promise either has been fulfilled or will be fulfilled. It is a firm foundation for hope!

2. Another great reason for hope is that we as believers have some things that will never fade away! He tells us of our "inheritance" that is "reserved in heaven." I may lose everything down here; but, praise God, I got something up there that I will never lose! For those thinking they may not make it there, Peter adds these words, *"Who are kept by the power of God..."* You can't beat that deal!

3. Peter gave us the *blessed hope,* as Paul calls it in Titus 2:13, of the Second Coming of Jesus. No matter how bad it gets down here, Jesus is coming again and will make everything all right! Tell that to people who ask you. He can come any minute to take us home! Peter said in I Peter 1:13 that the Second Coming should cause us to "hope to the end." Never lose hope!

4. We can also give *the Bible* as a reason for our hope to those that ask. Read I Peter 1:23: *"Being born again, not of corruptible seed, but of incorruptible, by the word of God, which liveth and abideth forever."* He is reminding people who are suffering and have lost everything that this Book is something that lasts forever -- the Word of God. Only eternal things can give eternal hopes. Note I Peter 1:24-25: *"For all flesh is as grass, and all the glory of man as the flower of grass. The grass withereth, and the flower thereof falleth away: But the word of the Lord endureth forever. And this is the word which by the gospel is preached unto you."* They still had God's Word, and so do we! I do not know exactly why, but I have found that fellow sufferers get a special love and desire for the Word in their darkest hours! Although I cannot exactly explain why, I know it is that way; you will too.

We do not need a special "word" from the Lord to comfort us in our trials. We have the Word of God! That is enough! I am so very saddened when I hear testimonies on Christian radio of hurting Christians who have heard a special word from the Lord in an almost audible voice assuring them to trust God. Usually it is spoken by a charismatic-type believer; but occasionally, some poor, ignorant follower of Christ, who knows little about the Bible, tells about God speaking to him in his hour of despair. They feel that was just what was needed, but it was not. You can hear the excitement in their voices which encourages others to seek the same experience. All they really needed is right in the Bible. All they needed to know was what the Scriptures say and where those wonderful promises to the "hurting" are found!

Someone might ask, "John, why make such a big deal about this kind of testimony?" Here are the reasons why:

1. The hurting person who hears that testimony thinks that he needs a voice if he is ever going to recover from his pain. He is listening more for a voice than searching in the Scriptures. What a tragedy that anyone might turn his attention to seeking voices instead of seeking verses!

2. What happens to the hurting person who never hears that voice (so definite and distinct that he knows it was God's)? Is he going to live in disappointment because he did not hear the voice? There need not be any disappointment for any hurting person who rightly divides and applies the principles of the Word of God to his life!

3. I cringe to hear such testimonies because they exalt experience and a voice above the inspired Word of God. One such testimony brought "amen's" and "praise the Lord's" from the host and a very scary comment: "That's what God wants to do for all of His children, and that's what we prophesy will happen to those who follow our teaching of faith." You will not find that in the Bible! If their goal in teaching is to get people to have those kinds of experiences, then their ministry is not based on the Word of God! I know that sounds rather straightforward. I mean for it to be! That teaching hurts people; it does not help them. I do not want to be unkind toward some of the followers of charismatic teachers who are so confused and often deceived by those espousing false teachings. These dear, hurting people are reaching out to anything they can in their distress. Sadly, they have reached out

to some false teachers and have not yet discerned that. I want my ministry, however, to lead people to the Scriptures and all that God has for them in His Word, nothing more and nothing else. No voices, just verses! Do not be fooled by the fact that they say a few things right. All false teachers say some things right, or no one would be fooled by them. Even one of Job's friends, whom the Lord condemned in the latter part of the book, said something which was quoted later in the Bible itself. Yet, he spoke many things that were not right. (Job 5:17 and Hebrews 12:5-6)

I remember a dear lady making a statement to me after hearing me preach from a passage I dearly love, Psalm 34. I love that passage for many reasons; for one reason, it is an invitation to taste of God's goodness. She said, "Brother John, I love Psalm 34 so much now. I have drawn such comfort and encouragement from it when I am hurting and having problems. The whole book of Psalms has become a great source of help since you came to our church and preached from that chapter and some of the other Psalms." This was spoken some weeks after my being there. I left her with something far greater than the encouragement to seek a voice! People need verses much more than voices or visions! The verses of God's Word will always be there for them.

I want to throw in a few more important principles from I Peter before I finish my book:

1. As Peter closed the epistle in chapter 5, he addressed the elders or pastors. He gave the job of shepherding the dear people to the pastors. He referred to the Christians as sheep by describing them as a "flock" in verse 2. He told the pastors to feed the flock. That is important! Hurting people need pastors. They need a church where there are other sheep and a pastor who feeds them the Word of God. A pastor that feeds them is

103

more important than any other person, with the exception of the Lord Himself, of course.

Being fed the Word is more important to the hurting than being fed any other information. Hurting people that feed on psychology or counseling without the support of a church and a man of God teaching them the Word will never recover fully. I am not saying that you will never receive any help from other sources, but I am saying that you need a church home and a good pastor to teach you the Word of God.

2. Peter also reminded them that God cares when they are hurting. He still cares today! Read I Peter 5:7: *"Casting all your care upon him; for he careth for you."* He wants all our cares or worries, not just some of them. He wants them all -- big, little, and everything in-between to be cast or thrown upon Him. Hurting people are often tempted to think that God does not care when they hurt, but He does. Throw your burdens on the Lord right now. He wants them!

3. Peter also warned them to be careful because the devil is after them. Read the warning in verse 8. *"Be sober, be vigilant; because your adversary the devil, as a roaring lion, walketh about, seeking whom he may devour."* Here he pictures the devil as a lion hunting us down. I would venture to say that Peter thought of how Satan had attacked him after being warned by Christ in Luke 22:31: *"Simon, Simon, behold, Satan hath desired to have you, that he may sift you as wheat."* By the time Satan was done, Peter had denied the Lord three times. That is being devoured!

Remember that Peter described us as sheep in this passage. Sheep are no match for lions, but lions are no match for shepherds! Now Jesus is described here as the "Chief Shepherd." If we stay close to Jesus, we are safe. Our pastors (shepherds) can protect us when they have God's power, just as young lad David protected his daddy's sheep from a bear and a lion!

I believe God had already assured these dear Christians

that their souls were safe earlier in I Peter. I do not believe that the devil can devour the souls of believers, but he can devour their testimony and many other things other than their soul. Besides, the word *soul* is not found here. Do not read something into it that is not there. Why did he give this warning? I think it is because the devil works especially hard on hurting Christians. God was saying to be extra careful when you are hurting and to not let the devil take advantage of you at that time! The devil loves to attack Christians when they are down! He commands in the very next verse to "resist" the devil. James assures us in James 4:7, *"Submit yourselves therefore to God. Resist the devil, and he will flee from you."* Thank God Satan has to flee when we resist him! Do not feel like you have to give in to the devil and temptations when you are hurting.

4. One final principle found in this book is found in the last part of verse 5: *"...knowing that the same afflictions are accomplished in your brethren that are in the world."* One of the great dangers for hurting people is to think they are the only ones that have ever hurt in that way. God said there are others who are hurting like you all over the world. You are not alone. So do not think, "Poor me, nobody has it as bad as I do." Do not feel sorry for yourself thinking that nobody else has ever had it as bad as you. The truth is that there are many dear Christians in this world who love the Lord and have it much worse than you.

There are Christians all over this world who will have little to eat and will suffer the most awful abuses at the hands of others that would be hard for us to even imagine. Knowing and hearing how some of them came through their ordeals with faith intact encourages me. They have much more to worry about than many of us will ever know. Are you sick? So are they, yet many of them will have to suffer terribly because of poor health care or none at all.

I have read books written by hurting people who want to reach out to those hurting around them. Some of them say that it is not good to ever remind the hurting person that somebody has it worse than he does. I disagree to some extent with that condemnation. I do not think that it is always wrong or detrimental to remind others that other people do have it worse than they have it. I think it depends on how it is said and how such comparisons are used.

Peter reminded them here that others were going through the things they were going through. I remember hearing of others who went through some of the things I suffered. I felt that if they could make it through, perhaps I could, too! God holds up Job for us to learn from. It is not wrong to wonder how Job made it through after having ten children killed, losing everything, having his wife and friends turn against him, and being covered in painful boils. I thank God for holding this man up and for giving us the words that Job spoke in his weak times as well as in his strong times. Job did make it through. So can you and I!

I have a very dear friend Evangelist Tom Williams, whose dear wife was devastated by meningitis many years ago. I have spoken in services where she was present in her wheelchair with her nurse at her side listening to her husband preach. Her life story has challenged people all over the world. Bro. Williams's courage, love, and grace has been used of God to inspire us all. As for me, I always bow my head, sometimes with tears, and secretly thank God for sparing me some of the effects she has suffered. I wish it had never happened to her, but it has. God uses it to remind me how fortunate I am. God uses Brother Tom to show us that He can give grace in the face of such a trial. I hope that people who see the condition I am in, will be encouraged if they are fortunate enough to have escaped some of the problems that I face. Maybe somebody who faces an occasional tension headache, which can be relieved by a few over-the-counter medications, will stop and say, "Thank you, Lord," realizing that some of us face headaches so terrible that we roll on the floor begging God to let the narcotic take effect

> *We can learn to live joyfuly even with pain and disabilities! We can draw strength from others.*

quickly for some relief.

I could tell of another dear brother in Christ who went through an awful experience with the fiery death of his two precious children while he was at work. The circumstances involving their death were shocking. Yet this man has gone on not only to live, but also to live for God. He is actually involved in a building ministry that helps churches and Christian organizations all over America. You can go on, and you can go on with His peace and grace!

Now, I am not saying that we should all go around telling others how bad things are in order to help them. No, but neither should we hide how God is helping us get through problems joyfully, even though we do suffer greatly at times. Notice I said "joyfully." We can learn to live joyfully even with pain and disabilities! We can draw strength from others.

Choosers Not Losers

One of the saddest things I have found about hurting people is that some think that they are just losers. They even, at times, think they are born losers. I disagree totally with that attitude. Nobody is born a loser! I am sure I have probably heard this somewhere, but I say it often. "Nobody is born a loser. Everybody is born a chooser." Then I add, "Whether you are a winner or loser depends on what you choose!" We all must choose to win, and the choices are made every day.

We must choose Christ to be a winner! We must choose to receive Him. We must choose Him to save, forgive, and keep us. We must choose Him to give us grace for our trials and heartaches. Sometimes it is choosing between Christ and drugs. Sometimes it is choosing Christ's way over the world's way of dealing with our problems, pains, and plans. Sometimes the choices are very difficult. There are times we must choose to believe His promises and words even when it does not seem possible or when we feel so void and empty of any emotion.

It is not easy to believe without emotions, but it is possible. We like to "feel" before we believe. I know some disagree, but I believe that we can believe even when we do not feel like it. Sometimes people say, "I just feel like it's true!" when speaking of their beliefs. That is not a good rule at all. You should not have to feel anything in order to believe. I would love to tell you that the joyful, happy feelings will always follow believing, but I cannot use the word *always*. I can say *many times* or *eventually*, but not *always*. Sometimes pains inflict such emotional numbness upon us that happy feelings do not surface for a period of time.

The word *always* can be used when speaking of God's strength. I can use the word *always* with strengthening. You will always derive strength from believing His Word. Strength, at times, is just a quiet inner peace, like a soft whisper in your ear, reminding you that you have done the right thing by believing and trusting God. God honors such raw faith. Everybody wants a "feel-good" faith, one that just makes you feel good the instant you believe God's Word. Oh yes, I know faith can make you feel good, but that is not its only purpose; feeling good is not even its greatest reward.

Do not get me wrong about faith. Faith can make you feel good by rewarding you with the assurance that you are forgiven, saved, and on your way to heaven. It feels good to know these wonderful truths. It also feels good to know that we are saved "by grace through faith" and we are now God's own children. But faith, no matter how strong it is, does not always make us feel good immediately. Sometimes life has been shattered, or the body is raging in pain.

Faith can be the beginning of the healing process that is sometimes so painfully slow. When I crushed my finger one day working on a project at our church youth camp, it took many weeks to heal. A crushed heart or wounded spirit can take some time to heal, also. A bruised faith may take time to heal before it is not so sensitive to the "touch" or a spiritual "bump." I find people who are deeply bruised in life. Bruises are actually just outward signs of inward pains. The damage is actually below the surface of the skin, but the bruise just shows us where it is. Faith goes below the surface to bring healing.

Choose to be a winner. I guarantee that all those who

have been born again are born winners! Do not get the idea that you have just always been a loser, and that is all you will ever be. No! No! God has made you to be a winner in life. I do not mean that you will have an easy, happy life. No, winners in all areas of life have losses at times. We call great athletes winners even though they lose in their sport many times over a lifetime. We have all known business people who have lost everything only to later rise to the top. Sure, you have lost at times; that does not make you a loser. Sure, your health problems and family problems have been difficult hurdles for you, but that does not mean you cannot choose to be what God wants you to be -- a winner!

I thank God for those who have chosen to be winners, in spite of the many difficulties hurled at them. The writings and testimony of Joni Erickson Tada, a quadriplegic, have meant so much to me. A dear evangelist by the name of Tim Lee preaches for God all over the world, even though he lost both legs in Vietnam when he stepped on a land mine. When I see him in that Marine uniform preaching, I am glad he did not just come home from the war and hide away in self-pity. I am sure both of them were tempted to do that. They chose to live and win! Will you?

You Cannot Take Happiness out of My Vocabulary

1 believe with all my heart that it is right both Biblically and morally for Christians to lay claim to being happy! I believe it so much that my next book is going to be devoted to that very subject. In it, I plan to enlist a host of greatly admired Christians of the past to support the fact that Christians can be happy, as well as joyful. Some people may be scratching their heads right now saying, "Who would question that?" There are voices in every field of learning that challenge that right, although our Constitution guarantees the right to "pursue happiness." For the Christian, however, it will take more than a man-made document, no matter how important it may be, to make us feel it is right to pursue happiness.

I am not sure even the Bible gives us the right to "pursue" happiness, but it sure does give us the right to be happy! I had one pastor kindly correct me for speaking "too much," as he described it, on Christians being happy. He stated that Christians should not be happy, just joyful. He further stated that since he defined happiness as being based solely on happenings, it is not something we should seek to have. "Joy is much better," he said. "So why should we want to be happy?" Now, I am the last person in the world that should be challenging learned pastors, but I see all kinds of Biblical support for Christians being happy as well as joyful! Why can't we have both? Read these wonderful Scriptures:

Deuteronomy 33:29: "*Happy art thou, O Israel: who is like unto thee, O people saved by the LORD, the shield of thy help, and who is the sword of thy excellency! and thine enemies shall be found liars unto thee; and thou shalt tread upon their high places.*"

Job 5:17: "*Behold, happy is the man whom God correcteth: therefore despise not thou the chastening of the Almighty:*"

Psalm 144:15: "*Happy is that people, that is in such a case: yea, happy is that people, whose God is the LORD.*"

Psalm 146:5: "*Happy is he that hath the God of Jacob for his help, whose hope is in the LORD his God:*"

Proverbs 3:13: "*Happy is the man that findeth wisdom, and the man that getteth understanding.*"

Proverbs 29:18: "*Where there is no vision, the people perish: but he that keepeth the law, happy is he.*"

John 13:17: "*If ye know these things, happy are ye if ye do them.*" (Jesus said this!)

Acts 26:2: "*I think myself happy, king Agrippa, because I shall answer for myself this day before thee touching all the things whereof I am accused of the Jews:*"

I could go on, but I think it is clear to see that we can be a happy people when we love, trust, obey, and walk with the Lord. I actually heard one preacher preach that Christians should never talk about being happy, only joyful, because we should not confuse the world.

I think it is confusing to the world to relegate happiness to the heathens! I think it is a discredit to Christ to put down happiness for the holy! I do not think that dear man was miserable, nor do I think I should attack him for his position, but I can certainly voice my belief that only Godly people can truly be happy!

We can be happy when difficult things are happening because we have Christ for every problem. Have you ever seen a happy, sick person? I have, and I also strive to be one.

I picked up a newspaper called *USA TODAY* in the airport on Monday, December 9, 2002. It caught my attention because in large letters on the front page were these words: "What Makes People Happy?" I wanted to read their view on what makes people happy. I was never so disappointed in my life! They made this claim as a subtitle: "Psychologists Now Know." What a claim! They featured a man whom they called "Dr. Happiness." He was described as a "happy guru" named Ed Diener, who has done extensive studies in the field of happiness. Here is what was so shocking and disappointing: God was not mentioned one time in the article! Religion was not even mentioned. Religious terms were used, such as "friends" and "forgiveness," but not faith or faith in God!

Now, the doctor may have brought out faith in some of his books, but he did not mention it in the article to literally hundreds of thousands of readers of the *USA TODAY.* I have not researched his other written material to find out if he says it in any of them. I am not saying he is void of faith or has not belief in God. But how can you highlight what makes people happy without even mentioning God? It is impossible! The whole tenor of the article to me was that happiness can be found in people, beauty, relationships, or satisfaction with your life, job, etc., without even acknowledging God. I think that is a false impression! Based on what the Bible says in just the verses I have listed above, happiness cannot be found without knowing and obeying our Maker and Creator!

That is why Christians have the "edge" on happiness,

because we can be happy even when our families fail us. The Lord knows that many dear Christians live in dysfunctional homes or in no homes at all. Sad to say, there are some families that are not "there" for one another. Christians can still have joy and happiness when their jobs fail and their health fails! The reason why is because we know and serve a living, joyful, loving, and forgiving God who knows us by name! Watch out! I feel happiness coming on!

I have coached some basketball in our small Christian school since my illness. I have learned something big: winners are happier than losers! We can be happy because we are on the winning team with Christ!

I love the words of the troubled prophet Habakkuk in that small book named after him in the Bible. He was troubled over the fact that God would use wicked nations to chastise His own people. He felt that these nations were much worse than Israel. He did not understand God's ways, and God was not explaining Himself to him. The first two words in the book are "*The burden...*" The second verse shows frustration. "*O, Lord, how long shall I cry, and thou wilt not hear!*" I love the book so much because of how he ended it. Even though God had not explained Himself, he said in Habakkuk 3:17-18, "*Although the fig tree shall not blossom, neither shall fruit be in the vines; the labour of the olive shall fail, and the fields shall yield no meat; the flock shall be cut off from the fold, and there shall be no herd in the stalls: Yet I will rejoice in the LORD, I will joy in the God of my salvation.*" Joy and happiness in the hard times are what is needed today!

A winner is not a person who never gets down when things are tough. He just does not stay down. I do not think sheer determination alone can get you back up emotionally or physically. Determination cannot repair a severed spine, but it can help you work harder at becoming better at everyday tasks. I do not talk much about my determination; I spend most of my time talking about grace. God is the One that picks up the down-hearted person, and faith is what asks Him to do it. In spite of what some say, **faith does not always get healing; but it always gets help - God's help.**

I am a terrible basketball player now because of my physical limitations, but I would not be afraid to play a game of two-on-two basketball with anybody if I had a young Michael Jordan on my team! If nothing else, I could knock people out of his way as he went to the goal. Faith puts God on our team or puts us on His team! He cannot lose, and neither can you when you are on His team!

Now, allow me to carry this a little farther. I can be fouled, knocked down by the opponents, or hurt, but I will win because God cannot be stopped! *"If God be for us, who shall be against us?"* (Romans 8:31) This is not suggesting that if God is on our side we will not have anybody against us. All of Scripture clearly tells us otherwise. It is just saying that it does not matter who is against us, we still win! All those against us will fail in the end!

> *A winner is not a person who never gets down when things are tough. He just does not stay down.*

The Great Experiment

I draw comfort from the Scriptures more than anything else. I have studied many of the main words that deal with help and hope from the Lord. One such passage gave me a beautiful thought. Romans 5:1-5: *"Therefore being justified by faith, we have peace with God through our Lord Jesus Christ: By whom also we have access by faith into this grace wherein we stand, and rejoice in hope of the glory of God. And not only so, but we glory in tribulations also: knowing that tribulation worketh patience; And patience, experience; and experience, hope: And hope maketh not ashamed; because the love of God is shed abroad in our hearts by the Holy Ghost which is given unto us."*

He starts by saying why he would "glory" in tribulations in verse 3. Did you know *glory* is also translated *joy* and *rejoice*? He could rejoice in tribulations because he saw the good that came from them. Can we?

The word *worketh* is translated *cause* on another occasion. So tribulations work or cause patience in our lives. God knows we all could use more patience. Even if it is hard to come by, it is still a very precious gift. God refers to the "patience of Job" in James 5:11 with its rewards. There is great reward in patiently waiting on

My love for word studies in the Bible revealed a golden nugget of truth to me. The word *experience* is also translated *experiment* in II Corinthians 9:13. What a great thought! We are God's experiment to the world. I sure do not want to end up as "an experiment gone bad." What brings the "experience" as an "experiment" is tribulation.

Now, the patience produces the experience. We will experience God's grace, peace, strength, and power when we patiently bear our burdens. That is not easy, but it is rewarding. When the world sees us patiently trusting and waiting on God, they will want to know the Lord. God is using us in a great experiment. When I have gone to our school to watch science experiments, usually everything used in the experiment is either crushed, broken, heated, or ground in the process. So it is with us! For the experiment to be a success, we must be broken, crushed, placed in the fire to be heated, and at times ground to pieces.

A wonderful truth in this passage is also found in verse 5 where it speaks of God's love being "shed abroad" in our hearts. I think God shows extra love to His children in their experiences and experiments. I have felt His love so much during my illnesses. I love Him dearly! The word *shed* is also translated "poured out" and "gushed out" elsewhere. It is good to think that God pours His love on us in our trials, and His love comes gushing out! Wow! Please, Lord, make your love gush out of my life when I am broken!

Just like students around a professor in a college laboratory are watching him doing an experiment, the world is standing around watching God perform His experiment on you and me. They cannot see Him, but they can watch and observe the results. Will we come out all right? Will we prove to be the right and real stuff? Will they be able to see that those with the Lord can come through anything and still love, trust, and praise Him? I sure hope so!

He also states in verse 4 that after experience comes hope! It does not leave us without hope. There is always hope, no matter how long or hard the experiment may be! There is hope for you even if you have failed parts of the test. You can still come through with "flying colors." No professor quits just because of a failure in the classroom. You can be sure that the heavenly Professor never gives up on us, even if we have failed before! Go back to Him and say, "Lord, try again. Help me this time to get it right!" He will! One of the greatest psalms for discouraged and depressed Christians is Psalm 42. David said in Psalm 42:3, *"My tears have been my meat day and night..."* He was seemingly confused, as depressed people often get, and asked in Psalm 42:5, *"Why art thou cast down, O my soul? and why art thou disquieted in me?..."* He repeated this question in Psalm 42:11. Many times hurting people really cannot figure out just what it is that is making them so depressed.

Thankfully, he admitted it to God in Psalm 42:6. *"O my God, my soul is cast down within me..."* Yet he never loses hope! He reminds himself *"...hope thou in God..."* in Psalm 42:5. Tell God how you really feel and do not lose hope! I love what this depression and heartache caused David to do -- thirst for God! He says in Psalm 42:2, *"My soul thirsteth for God, for the living God..."* He was not thirsting for things from God, but for God Himself! How thirsty are you for God? That reminds me of what Jesus preached in Matthew 5:6: *"Blessed are they which do hunger and thirst after righteousness: for they shall be filled."*

Note that Jesus did not say He would bless those who would just "like" or "want" righteousness; He said "hunger" and "thirst." I believe that the reason most Christians are not filled and blessed is because they are not really hungry and thirsty enough yet! I am not so sure that those tears David mentioned in this Psalm were only for self-pity. I think some of those tears were evidence of just how much he wanted God in his life! Have you shed any tears lately seeking Him in your life?

Seeing the Fourth Man in the Fire

*T*here is a wonderful story, which many people know, in the third chapter of Daniel. It is about three Hebrew children, who are better known by the names Shadrach, Meshach, and Abednego. They chose to disobey the command of the heathen king that demanded that everyone bow down to his golden image. Even after the king threatened to cast them into a fiery furnace if they refused to serve or worship his image, they answered, *"If it be so, our God whom we serve is able to deliver us from the burning fiery furnace, and he will deliver us out of thine hand, O king. But if not, be it known unto thee, O king, that we will not serve thy gods, nor worship the golden image which thou hast set up."*

That took courage and grace! After they said that, the furnace was not the only thing hot! The king was burning up with anger! He had them heat the furnace seven times hotter than it would normally be heated just to cook those guys "good and proper!" The devil gets mad when God's people take a stand for the Lord; are you glad he is not the one in control?

Because the king was so mad, he could not see or think straight; he hurried the men throwing these Godly young men into the fire. The rush cost the lives of those men who obeyed the king's command. I wonder how many people the devil has destroyed while he was trying to hurt God's people. Does he care? No!

Then King Nebuchadnezzar was shocked by what he saw next. He looked in the furnace at the young men and saw a fourth Person in there with them! He described that fourth Person as *"...like the Son of God."* Now, I do not know how he knew that term or description, and I do not have to know how. I just know that he saw our Lord Jesus in that fire with His children. The Lord Jesus spends a lot of time in the fire with His children! I am not so sure, but that might be one of His favorite places. Note this next statement: the world sees Jesus when they look at us in the fire! The king was not looking for Jesus. He was looking at the three Hebrew children and just happened to see Jesus there with them. The world is most likely going to see the Lord when they see us walking with Him in the fire!

I thought this was interesting concerning the word *fourth.* Did you know that it was the fourth watch of the night when Jesus came walking on the stormy water to his disciples in the midst of the sea? The story is told in Matthew 14:22-33. The fourth Man came in the fourth watch, the darkest hour just before dawn. Christ comes to us in our darkest hour. They say the fourth watch is between 3 to 6 a.m. If you are in the midst of your darkest, coldest hour, look for Jesus!

According to verse 26, the disciples did not even recognize Him at first. *"It is a spirit..."* Storms and trouble can distort our view of Christ if we are not careful. Be careful not to let your hurting distort your view of Christ so much that it hinders you from seeing Him come to you in your storms and trials!

Are we the kind of Christians these three Hebrew children were? Do we take a stand for the Lord and right? Do we stand not only publicly, but also privately? If we were asked, "Is it true... do not ye serve my gods, nor worship the golden image which I have set up?" could we speak with a clear conscience? The king wanted to know more than whether or not they would bow down to the image right then. He also wanted to know if they served his gods or not. When their public test came, they did not bow because they were not secretly serving false gods. What we are secretly will show up when we are tested openly. Jesus could walk openly in fellowship with these men who stood openly with Him!

What we are secretly will show up when we are tested openly.

Enthusiasm

1 love the word *enthusiasm*! I found out that it is made up of two Greek words *en* and *theos* (in God). Enthusiasm comes from God being in us! Saved people should be the most enthusiastic people in the world. The Apostle Paul loved to remind us that we have God's Spirit living in us! I Corinthians 3:16 says, *"Know ye not that ye are the temple of God, and that the Spirit of God dwelleth in you?"*

I know we all hurt at times; but with God in us, we always have hope. We know we can overcome any sin or Satanic attack because the Bible says in I John 4:4, *"Ye are of God, little children, and have overcome them: because greater is he that is in you, than he that is in the world."* Our biggest problems are with ourselves. My worst enemy is John Bishop, not anybody else. God wants me to be like Christ, and I fall so far short! Yet we also know that Paul described God as living in us, not only as the Holy Spirit, but also as Christ in us. Colossians 1:27 says, *"To whom God would make known what is the riches of the glory of this mystery among the Gentiles; which is Christ in you, the hope of glory."*

God wants to even use our hurts from others. Do you understand that God allows people to do things that can hurt us very deeply, either physically, emotionally, or both, to open doors for us to help others? I am director and founder of a youth camp that has over 2,500 campers per season. We have around ninety churches that come there each summer. There were some men who disagreed with me over handling a camp situation. God allowed two men to hurt me very deeply when they verbally attacked me, judged my motives, and misused a Scripture passage to do it. Their letters hurt me deeply, but what hurt me most was the way they used a Scripture. True Bible believers having a disagreement over non-doctrinal issues should never use the Scriptures against one another. I complained to one person, and God quickly convicted me.

Then the Lord enabled me to respond in a Scriptural way that helped me and helped others. At first, I wanted to respond in anger with a letter using some Scripture that could be used to attack their motives and methods. They used a Scripture in which Paul used the word *doctrine*, when it was not a doctrinal issue. Paul also described those he referred to as ones who were not serving the Lord Jesus at all. I wanted to hurt back. They could have used that Scripture and added something like, "We are not at all saying that you are not a servant of Christ, but we disagree with how you are doing it." Or, "We know you are doctrinally true, but disagree with how you are applying the Scripture in this instance." The only ones who have ever accused me of doctrinal error have been those from cults or fringe groups, never my own brethren. Even though I wish I had handled the issue better, I was really trying to do the right thing and not for selfish reasons as they stated.

However, God allowed me to see some areas in my life which I needed to correct as a result of the disagreement ,and I did correct them. God used it to show me some weaknesses and make some things right. I shared some of my hurt with some of the dear people of our church family and requested their prayers. I wept for days. The pain was real. In some respects, more real than the headaches I have. (I am purposely being vague about details so others will not know who is involved. Remember I stated ninety

128

churches a year use our facilities. I mention this, so it would not be evident to anybody who I am referring to.)

Sometimes we throw everything that somebody says to us away because they may say something wrong, unkind, or in a wrong way. I am learning that when God allows such attacks, He is allowing them for a reason. God allowed Paul to be mistreated and misunderstood not only by the world, but also by church members, like at Corinth. He stated in II Corinthians 6:11-13, *"O ye Corinthians, our mouth is open unto you, our heart is enlarged. Ye are not straitened in us, but ye are straitened in your own bowels. Now for a recompence in the same, (I speak as unto my children,) be ye also enlarged."* Paul was hurting because of some of the false accusations that some people in this church had made about him and his ministry even though he had done so much for them.

In verse 8 of the same chapter, Paul shared how he had to face evil reports and be called a deceiver by the very people he loved and even birthed into the kingdom! Paul's motives were being questioned. I know a little how Paul felt. Christians, are we better than the Apostle Paul? That is why he was saying in the verses above that he loved them so much; he was just pleading for them to love him in return. Yet Paul has encouraged every preacher since that time who has been hurt by those he loves to keep loving them and not get bitter. God used the right response in my life to help several people who eventually came to me later and said God used it to encourage them in a similar battle. We had two wonderful families come to our church when they saw how I responded to my trial. Good came from it! One Christian lady shared a wonderful testimony with me about how God used my situation at just the time they too were going through a very similar trial. God's timing was right on target! I feel sorry for those men, and I can honestly say I love them and pray for them.

I shared the above story because some people feel like they do not know real pain unless they have gone through some traumatic, physical suffering. Paul felt the pain of suffering rejection, and misunderstanding was very real to Paul -- real enough to cause him to write much Scripture, here and in other epistles, about the way he felt at the hands of other Christians who hurt him. I was amazed at how many times people hurt or disappointed him. He mentioned Demas as forsaking him in II Timothy 4:10; Alexandar did him "much evil" in verse 14; and even all "men forsook me" in verse 6. Yet he prayed it would not be "laid to their charge"! How do you pray for those who have hurt or disappointed you? Read the book of II Timothy as he named two men of Asia who turned away from him! Yet he mentioned Onesiphorus as making it up. God always has His helpers! Please remember that Paul never quit because of his hurt. Please do not quit either! It is exciting to see trials as opportunities to grow and bring about good!

Now, let us leave Paul's story and return to Peter's. Peter said that Christ is in us and that He is coming back for us one day! Peter used the principle of the second coming as a reason for hope for his hurting audience which was "scattered." Note what he said in I Peter 1:13, *"Wherefore gird up the loins of your mind, be sober, and hope to the end for the grace that is to be brought unto you at the revelation of Jesus Christ."* He is coming back for us. I love the beautiful thought in Revelation 21:4, *"And God shall wipe away all tears from their eyes; and there shall be no more death, neither sorrow, nor crying, neither shall there be any more pain: for the former things are passed away."* That verse says that God Himself will wipe away our tears! It will not be angels or anybody else, but God Himself! That touches me so much!

I remember times when my Donna would wipe away my tears when I was hurting so much. Nobody could wipe my tears away with the love and tenderness that My Donnas has. I look forward to the day when God will tenderly and lovingly wipe my tears away! He is such a good God and a good Father!

Until then, let us be like Paul once again. Paul wanted to be known as one who is a helper of the joy of others. II Corinthians 1:24 says, *"Not for that we have dominion over your faith, but are helpers of your joy: for by faith ye stand."* Are we helping others find joy? One way of doing this is to strengthen the faith of the believers, as Paul stated, *"..by faith ye stand."* In order to have joy, people need a faith on which they can stand.

Note that Paul said "your joy" in the above reference. He did not say "his joy," but theirs. You have to have some joy of your own before you can be helped. Do you have any joy in knowing and trusting in Christ? Until you have the joy of knowing Christ personally, which means you have been forgiven and given a home in heaven, nobody can help your joy. You must have some first; then I and other dear Christians can help your joy grow even more.

I often wondered why I had so many fears early in my illness. It seemed everything made me fearful. Now that I have had time, I can retain some things in memory, although it is still limited how much I retain. With my loss of memory, I did not have the Scriptures in my mind to use and lean on or draw comfort from when fearful things happened to me. Now that I have some of those wonderful promises in my mind to draw from, I have something to focus on and rely on when those fears well up in me. Please do not take that for granted!

Am I normal? I am a long way from it if you mean am I like most people. I am not like most people, but that is all right! I do things that normal people do not do. I have sat for hours just watching life around me, thinking and thanking God for my beautiful part of earth. I have lain in the grass for so long that I dozed off watching ants carry their food with the help of their friends. If I have to stop such things to be normal, I think I will just stay the way I am! I love being able to be so utterly dependent on God that I picture Him just holding me in His arms like a baby lamb.

At the airport the other evening, I saw how wonderful a dear child with great physical and mental limitations can be to us all. She was there in her wheelchair with her father standing behind her. Suddenly what must have been a sister or dear friend came walking toward her! She smiled and loudly said, "Hi!" She proclaimed her happiness so excitedly and loudly that all of us standing around looked that way. I saw some people shake their heads as if to say, "The poor child is so pitiful." Others even gave a look of disdain. I smiled really big and said to myself, "Aren't her excitement and smile worth the whole trip? That is the purest form of love I have seen in a long time!" That beats "normal" any day!

------ ❦ ------

I believe pain is something God has called me to. You have already noted my love for the book of First Peter. Peter reminds these hurting people of one other thing -- their calling! The Christian life not only begins with a call, but also ends with a call to come up to heaven and join Him. We call this time the rapture. Really and truly, however, we must hear God's call in all areas of our lives for the rest of our lives. Peter reminds them of their call to holiness in chapter 1 and verse 15. Dear hurting Christian, God is more interested in holiness than happiness, although He can produce both in our lives!

He reminds them that they have been called out of darkness "into His marvelous light." After doing so, he tells them to live like people called out of the darkness of this world! Our lives should be different because of God's calling. Do not ever forget that God's calling may include or allow darkness of depression, doubt, or despair; but we will never be without His glorious light! One of the greatest things to scatter depression and dark feelings is light; and God says we have it!

Knowing that at this time God is calling me to be a faithful, loving servant while I live with pain makes it so much easier to bear. I do not mean a grit-your-teeth and bear-it attitude, but a deep-down gratitude in bearing my trials. I also know the One calling me has been there before me. His suffering was totally unjust and undeserving, but look what great good has come from it! Great good can come from ours, too! Paul loved to refer to himself many times in his epistles as one who was called! I can see why that was a great motivating force in his life.

You see a "call" is more personal than a "command." In order for someone to hear your call, you have to personally single them out. In *Strong's Concordance,* the first definition for the Greek word translated *called* in Romans 8:28 is "invited." This Greek word is said to come from another Greek word translated as "invite." Although His callings do include demands, I think they mainly express desires. The Lord makes us an offer to follow Him and tells us a little of what we can expect by way of rewards and suffering. I want to answer the call clearly and lovingly: "YES, I will do it!"

Can you hear His call and invitation to follow Him and suffer with Him and even perhaps for Him? When God speaks, it is in a still, small voice. Do not listen for a loud call. Listen for a loving call to take up arms to fight for Him and suffer in His battle for souls. II Timothy 2:3 says, *"Thou therefore endure hardness, as a good soldier of Jesus Christ."*

Please remember something God said in James 5:11: *"Behold, we count them happy which endure."* Is it not wonderful that God put happiness and endurance in the same verse? Only God can put happiness and endurance together! He can do it in our lives also. Answering the call to endure is not surrendering to an unhappy, dull life but a happy life!

The Things That Have Happened unto Me

Paul wanted people to understand that the trials and problems he had been having were actually used of the Lord to do good things. Notice his words to the Philippians in Philippians 1:12. *"But I would ye should understand, brethren, that the things which happened unto me have fallen out rather unto the furtherance of the gospel."* What had he mentioned earlier in this epistle that he could be referring to? In verse 7 of this same chapter, Paul referred to his "bonds." He was not talking about savings bonds. I assure you that. He is speaking of the imprisonment and harsh treatment that he had received from the enemies of Christ. He mentioned the bonds again in verse 13.

Notice he said "understand." He knew that it would be hard for some people to understand that good things can come from the so-called bad things that happen to Christians. He knew many of the Christians there would be thinking maybe Paul had done something wrong to deserve these kinds of trials and tribulation. He knew others might just be confused and wondering if God's plan had been messed up. Why would God allow this to happen to a man in the prime of his ministry? What are you doing, God? Does this sound familiar?

Paul is saying to the "prosperity gospel" crowd and the many other sincerely confused believers that misunderstand how God works through trials, "Let me show you how God has worked through this." Now none of us, especially me, can understand all the ways in which God works through trouble; but according to Paul, we can understand some things about it. What can we understand?

We can understand that through his bonds the wonderful message of Christ went clear to the "palace" and "in all other places." What a wonderful result of trials! What has happened as a result of my illness? I have been able to help more people than I ever did before my illness. God has opened doors for me to preach to more people than I have ever preached. Did I understand all these wonderful things would happen from meningitis at first? No, I am not sure I fully understand it now, but I understand more as I am going along in life. God is so good!

Do you understand that God allows people to do things that can hurt very deeply either physically, emotionally, or both that could open doors for you to help others? I hope I have illustrated that through those hurts I have received from others as well as my physical problems. Paul not only had his thorn in the flesh but also his thorny friends like we all have! Yet, he rejoiced that some were preaching Christ because of him, even if they did it for the wrong reasons! He made good people more bold to share their faith as they watched him respond correctly to his trials.

I like how Paul talked about making a choice. He said, "...what I shall choose..." You have a choice also. He wanted greatly to be home in heaven with the Lord (as many hurting people also desire), yet he wanted so much to stay here for "...your furtherance and joy of faith." How unselfish he was! Will you choose life over death to help others and bring them joy? He reminded them, "For unto you it is given in the behalf of Christ, not only to believe on him, but also to suffer for his sake; Having the same conflict which ye saw in me..." We do not deserve any better treatment than Paul!

Will we choose to love and live for others in response to our trials? Some of my trials have shown me some things about myself that God needed to change. I could not or would not have seen them before my trials. That is just one of many good things that trials have brought me. I believe I do love others more and try harder to bring joy to others' lives. We have to choose each day either self-pity or self-sacrifice. It is not only a daily choice; in painful times, it is also a choice made by the hour or even by the minute.

Why Didn't God?

eople have asked me why God did not do certain things certain ways if He is both good and all-powerful. People have asked me one question that is found in most books grappling with the issues of pain and suffering in the world: "Why didn't God make a perfect world without allowing temptation, Satan, or the possibility of sin?" Many who are much smarter and wiser than I have given some very good insight into answering that question. I will not give those ideas now, but I want to share a thought that helped a sincere seeker to find the Lord.

A fellow sufferer asked that very question. Here was the simple response that God used. I stated, "He is making a world just like that right now, one in which there will be no possibility of sin. No presence of Satan or temptation will ever be allowed in that world. It will be perfect forever!"

She asked with a surprised look, "What do you mean He is making it now?"

I stated, "He is working on the city now and has been for two thousand years! When He comes back, He will do away with this old earth and make a new one after He locks Satan up forever."

"Why didn't He do that to start with?" she asked.

I added, "I don't know, but are you going to miss out on it just because you don't know the answer to that one question? Are you going to miss out on a perfect world without any possibility of sin, sickness, disease, death, or pain simply because you don't know why God allowed such things in His first world?"

I assured her that God has invited everyone to this new world, but only those who receive His Son can go in. I said, "Please do not miss this wonderful, perfect world simply because you do not have an answer to such a question about God. Get in on His new world. Come through by trusting and receiving a wonderful Savior, Jesus Christ!"

She stated, "I never thought of it that way. I would be foolish to miss out of what will be a world we all long for!"

She got blessed assurance that day! Will you accept Him also? If you already have, please help me invite others to get in on this new world. He is preparing a place where all His children will live, laugh, and love forever!

How God Uses Suffering

od uses suffering for purifying us. Malachi 3:3 says, "And he shall sit as a refiner and purifier of silver: and he shall purify the sons of Levi, and purge them as gold and silver, that they may offer unto the LORD an offering in righteousness." When God wants to purify us and enable us in righteousness, He uses fire, the same thing used to purify metal. Peter referred to a trial as a "fiery trial" in I Peter 4:12; the word *trial* here is the Greek word *purosis*. The word is defined in the *Strong's Concordance* as "4448; ignition, i.e. (specially), smelting (figuratively, conflagration, calamity as a test):—burning, trial." Note that it is also translated "burning." Blessed fire rids me of anything that is not right and pure in my heart, motives, and life!

II. God uses suffering for preparing us. I want to use Joseph to illustrate this principle. Note what is said of Joseph in Psalms 105:17-19. *"He sent a man before them, even Joseph, who was sold for a servant: Whose feet they hurt with fetters: he was laid in iron: Until the time that his word came: the word of the LORD tried him."* God was using all these terrible things in Joseph's life to prepare him for the time He would use him.

Notice the phrase, "Until the time." God's timing allowed Joseph to suffer long and hard, but the rewards were so great. Joseph expressed his feelings in the name he gave his son, Manasseh. Genesis 41:51: *"And Joseph called the name of the firstborn Manasseh: For God, said he, hath made me forget all my toil, and all my father's house."* Manasseh means "forgetting." The joy of having a family and a child helped him forget all the years in prison, false accusations, and suffering. I love to tell others that the sheer joy of one second in heaven with Jesus will cause me to forget that I ever had any pain and suffering! God is preparing you through your trials for something bigger than you can ever imagine! Get excited and trust Him to show you one day! God has used meningitis to give me the greatest ministry opportunities I could ever imagine! He used five long years to get me ready -- I mean really long. However, I would not trade them for anything now because I see how He is working in my life to help hurting people! God is so good!

We must not confuse "greatness" with "bigness." I know I will never be able to be big, nor will I be great. A few big churches in size use me mainly because they love me, not because I can preach well. I know that. I consider it to be great when God uses me to reach a dear invalid who has given up on life.

Many years ago, I met a pastor by the name of Cliff Frink. God prepared Pastor Frink to help others years ago while he was in his teens. The car he was driving was hit by a concrete truck killing the three passengers. He alone survived. He went through very difficult and dark days as a result. He even contemplated suicide but, thankfully, realized that is never an answer. He surrendered to God's will and is now pastoring a great, thriving church in Florida. He wrote a tract telling of his struggles and victory. I preached for him in 2002. When I returned home after preaching for him, I received a phone call from a preacher I had just preached for recently. One of his teens had a terrible accident that resulted in the death of another man. I sent them several of Brother Cliff's tracts, and God used them! God used what had happened to bring good just like He said in Romans 8:28!

I am not suggesting God wanted the death of those teens in order to use Brother Cliff twenty years later, any more than He wanted the deaths of those innocent people killed by a falling tower mentioned in Luke 13:4-5. *"Or those eighteen, upon whom the tower in Siloam fell, and slew them, think ye that they were sinners above all men that dwelt in Jerusalem? I tell you, Nay: but, except ye repent, ye shall all likewise perish."* Some thought these people were terrible because something so bad had happened to them. Christ said, no, but that they had better repent. I think the reason why He said "repent" instead of "believe" while their hearts were still tender because of this tragedy was so they would turn to the Lord before their tears dried up. God did not want their deaths, but He used the incident to point others to the Lord! He does not tell us why it happened or whether He or the devil caused it. He just said, "Repent!" Do not worry about the theological problems this terrible incident poses; just repent. I wish people would stop arguing over how to explain the devastation of September 11, when those towers were destroyed with thousands of people, and just repent and get ready for the day of their own deaths! Why should I try to answer things about that tragedy that Jesus Himself did not answer?

III. God uses suffering for perfecting us. Hebrews 2:10: *"For it became him, for whom are all things, and by whom are all things, in bringing many sons unto glory, to make the captain of their salvation perfect through sufferings."* Christ was made perfect through His sufferings. We know that does not mean He was imperfect or sinful, because He was the sinless Son of God. God in the flesh could not sin! The perfecting of Him for His mission to save sinners was brought about through the things He suffered while walking and living on earth in the flesh and dying on the cross. I do not want to get in a great theological discussion that would be over my head, but Jesus did need something that only sufferings could bring to fulfill His mission.

I have two pastors in my life right now: my oldest son, Mark, and Dr. Eric Capaci, who pastors the church out of which we are a mission church. I love them both dearly. I have noticed that Dr. Capaci, who is one of the most dynamic, spirit-filled preachers I know, can preach to teens as well as he can to adults. I have him speak at our youth camp every year. He has a combination rarely found in men who are great preachers -- compassion and fire. Most men have one or the other. He has both, and it shows clearly when he talks to teens from broken homes or dysfunctional homes. The reason is this: he came from such a home himself. He tells about it every year in at least one message. He is always so respectful and thoughtful of both his parents when he does so. No bitterness toward either one ever rears its ugly head, just compassion and understanding. His brokenness touches the broken. He weeps one minute and shouts the next minute. He both cries and cries out in his messages. He is an awesome preacher, partly because he has experienced brokenness. Teens, please remember that God often uses trials and brokenness during the teenage years in preparation for great adulthood blessings and honor as He did in the life of Joseph.

My son Mark has been used of the Lord in our mission church. We have seen many come to the Lord, and God has given us tremendous growth in a short time. I found one of the "secrets" or reasons for this blessing one day when I stopped by the church to pray with my son. We knelt in his office to pray, and Mark wept over his people and souls. When we got up, I saw the tears still streaming down his eyes, and I thought: "This is why God is giving us this fruit. Brokenness!" One Sunday morning when he preached with brokenness on the subject of hell, seven precious adults got saved at the close of the service!

My middle son John David has been through some trying times in his life. I see it in his tenderness in dealing with others. He loves kids' ministries and preaches to them every week. Dear friend, God knows the only way of perfecting us is through suffering. We will never be complete or completely usable without it. If Christ needed sufferings, how much more do we? Are we willing to suffer in order to be and do all that God would have us to do?

IV. *God uses suffering for positioning us.* I want to use the life of Joseph once again to illustrate this. I love this thought! You're going to get a blessing from this; so hold on to your seat! Notice Joseph's words to his brothers in Genesis 50:20. *"But as for you, ye thought evil against me; but God meant it unto good, to bring to pass, as it is this day, to save much people alive."* His brothers were scared to death thinking that their brother, whom they sold as a slave because they were so jealous of him, was going to kill them now because he was a ruler. Joseph did not do so because he had seen the hand of God in what had happened, even though they were wrong in what they had done to him.

When he said, *"God meant it unto good...",* I think that we can conclude that God was using all this, including the evil done to him, to position him to save his family. Now, that was a very important family to save -- the Jewish race. Out of that race came Christ the Saviour of the world! God had to use all the sufferings, disgrace, and heartaches to put Joseph in a place and position in which to save His people and a lost and dying world! Is that not exciting? God uses suffering to position us for His work.

I know many preachers and could tell many stories of how God used suffering to put people where He wanted them to serve and save others. They would not have gone, had it not been for the suffering. I read about a dear Christian man who ended up in the hospital needing an emergency surgery. While in the hospital, he met and led to the Lord a very influential business man who has reached hundreds for the Lord! He testified that God put him in the hospital to reach that man and even others while staying there. Now do not go and get all messed up with details or doctrinal language about how or why God works. Just trust God to put you where He wants you, even if some suffering is involved.

My Donna tells me of an incident that happened to us early in our marriage. During the first year of our marriage, she had a miscarriage. I rushed her to the hospital in the middle of the night while we lived there in Bristol, Tennessee. While they were attending to her physical needs, she said I waited in the waiting room where other expectant dads were staying. There in the middle of the night while our hearts were broken, I took the time to lead a first-time daddy to Christ. I do not remember his name, of course, or anything about him, but my Donna has said that it was even worth the Lord taking our baby to heaven in order for that man to get saved. That is grace!

Please notice I said "baby!" I believe that was a baby in the womb, and that God can give and take away as He sees best! I believe God took our baby just at that time so I would be in that hospital with that dad at that hour, so I could lead him to Christ. Please do not put me in some theological category because I believe that. I just think that is Biblical thinking. I am very sure that other Christians and especially preachers could "word" what I want to say better than I. Perhaps my words may not be giving just exactly the right theological balance. Forgive me for my failure; I do truly believe that doctrine and theology are important. I am not like some writers that seem to disdain doctrinal truth in order to say what they want to say.

I want to be doctrinally true as well as "heartedly" true. I think I made that last word up! I sincerely want what I say to come from the heart yet be Biblically sound. My goal is to "speak the truth in love..." I know I am not smart enough to have at my grasp the correct words for all that I want to say, but I do try to be careful. I did not say, "God took your baby..." but I did say, "God took our baby..." I can say that and not be mad at Him. I can still say that He is always good and always right, knowing that loss and many other losses that I have experienced since that time. Maybe you cannot do that; but please try to realize that I think God could lovingly do something like that even though my wife shared that we were both very hurt and disappointed when it happened.

One day, I reached across the aisle of a jet on my way to preach a "God Is So Good Sunday" and handed a lady one of my testimony tracts. I usually say, "Would you read this some time to see how good the Lord has been to me and helped me?" She immediately started reading it and crying. I half-teasingly said, "I know it is not very good, but I didn't think it was that bad!" She looked at me with a tear-stained face and said, "Brother John, God put you and me here in these very seats because He knew I needed this tract! You see, I just lost my second and only remaining child to a gun accident just a few months ago. The doctors told us we must get away for our health, mentally and emotionally. God knows I needed to be reminded that God truly is good no matter what happens in this world!" I was able to minister encouragement to her and her husband on their trip for their hurting hearts! Thank you, Lord!

When suffering and trouble come, let this thought come to your mind: "Have I ended up in this place or around these people so that I can minister to them?" I truly believe God has used meningitis to position me to help hurting people. I do not think I would be where I am without the suffering. I know that men use me to preach, not because I can speak well, but because of what God in His grace has brought me through. God is so good, and it has been worth it all! If you have ended up in a hospital, a nursing home, a wheelchair, a broken home, a broken relationship, or a lonely place with a broken heart, God is positioning you for your greatest task. So get ready and start looking for that person or people God has given you to reach! God is so awesome!

V. God uses suffering for picturing His grace, love, and power.

I turn to John chapter 9 for this illustration. It is the story of a man born blind that Jesus and His disciples happened to see when Jesus "passed by." When the disciples saw him, they wondered why such a thing would be. They did what is all right for any of us to do--they asked the Lord about it. Now, they already had a pre-conceived ideal, which is always a hindrance to us when seeking God's will. Here is a part of the narrative in John 9:2-3: *"And his disciples asked him, saying, Master, who did sin, this man, or his parents, that he was born blind? Jesus answered, Neither hath this man sinned, nor his parents: but that the works of God should be made manifest in him."* They just knew it had to be somebody's sin that caused this, but Jesus said it was not sin at all. It was so that He could manifest His grace and power to others. He wanted to use this man as a picture or photograph of grace! Is not that a wonderful thought?

Let Us Quickly Understand Some Basic Things Here:

1. Children born with physical challenges are not the results of sins. Now, I know that if a mother uses drugs while she carries her child, she will do damage to her unborn child. That is just the simple matter of reaping and sowing; but please, never try to put a guilt trip on some parents who have a child born with limitations, even if the child is born out of wedlock. If it were a "principle" that all children born to parents who have sex outside of God's boundaries in marriage would be born with birth defects, it would always happen. It would not happen occasionally, but continually. It does not. You and I know that. A very small number of children born to unwed mothers have serious problems.

When it does happen, however, it is for a reason. God will use that child to do something special for Him! Now do not get the idea that this is only true if He heals them. No! He will use them the way they are if He chooses to do so! We do not know of any other children born blind whom Jesus healed. He may have. Let us not place blame unless some blame lies with a person who would purposely do harmful things to a baby. Let us be careful and sensitive in dealing with parents whose children are impaired or have died. God has used children that are impaired in different ways to touch me and others, even though He has not healed them. Their love and grace shines through their brokenness! God is so good to give them to us!

2. God can use any means He desires if He so chooses to heal. He does not always choose to heal. I know some will read that last statement and get mad, but I stand by it on Biblical grounds! I am not going to debate that right now or even later. Some say there are "two schools of thought" on that passage. I did not go to either one; so I am going to just share with you a fact. In this incident, God used "clay" and "spit." He did not always use that method.

I can just picture somebody being so dogmatic that this is the only way that they would name their church -- "The Exciting Fellowship of Spit and Clay!" I would not mind Jesus spitting in my eyes, but I am not sure I want anybody else doing it! Let God do things the way He wants and just rejoice and trust Him.

3. This man was still a sinner when he was healed. He had not been saved yet. God healed him in verse 6, and he believed in verse 38, *"And he said, Lord, I believe. And he worshipped him."* He was healed thirty-two verses before he got saved! This does not prove much for demanding faith as the only means of healing. I know that the Lord teaches in James 5:15, *"And the prayer of faith shall save the sick, and the Lord shall raise him up; and if he have committed sins, they shall be forgiven him."* I am not saying God does not use faith. I am just saying that some of you were healed of diseases and sicknesses before you were ever saved. God was sparing your life, so you could one day trust and know Him.

If God has spared your life, please trust and love Him as your very own. He was so good to keep you alive. You know you could have, and probably should have died; but God let you live. Now live for Him!

I remember some dear Christians who came by to visit me while I was still very sick. At the time, I was able to minister some to others by giving my testimony. They said they had a word for me from the Lord. Psalms 37:4-5: *"Delight thyself also in the LORD; and he shall give thee the desires of thine heart. Commit thy way unto the LORD; trust also in him; and he shall bring it to pass."* They said, "Brother John, if you will delight yourself in the Lord, God says He will give you the desires of your heart to be healed!" I knew they were sincere! I carefully studied in my mind what to say to them. This was my answer: "The desire of my heart is not to be healed; the desire of my heart is to be used, and God is giving me that every time I help some hurting person." I was not trying to be unkind to them, but I meant that with all my heart. I would rather be used than healed. Don't get me wrong. I would love it if I could have both -- to be healed and used. I am doing so much better that I try not to complain. O, how I would love for the Lord to take the pain away. I would love it if He would restore some bodily functions that would, in my opinion, help me to serve Him better. Yet, I know He knows best. I do not think He minds my asking, as long as I leave it in His hands. If I have progressed as far as He desires, I will gladly accept that if He will just use me.

If He will use this book in your hands, it is worth it. If He will use my testimony to encourage you to keep trying and serving God, it is worth it. If He would use my life story to win some soul for Him, it is worth it. It is worth it all if some dear young person will decide to go on living or some lonely, depressed saint will take hope for the future.

Author Unknown

That day will never break;
I'll pin my faith, my all in Him,
He maketh no mistake.

There's so much now I cannot see,
My eyesight is far too dim;
But come what may, I'll simply trust,
And leave it all to Him.

For by and by the mist will lift
And plain it all He'll make;
Through all the way, tho' dark to me,
He made not one mistake.

Remember: God is always good, and God is always right. Always!

What God's Goodness Can Do for You!

1. GIVE YOU A HOME IN HEAVEN!

Only a good God would offer to everyone a wonderful home in heaven free of charge. It's a gift. You must receive the gift, however, by receiving Jesus Christ as your personal Saviour. When you receive God's Son, you receive God's power and authority to be God's child and to live with Him in Heaven. *"But as many as received Him, to them gave he power to become the sons of God, even to them that believe on His name." (John 1:12)*

2. FORGIVE YOU OF ALL YOUR SINS!

Only a good God would forgive you of everything you ever did. The apostle Paul said that God's goodness should lead us to "repentance." (Romans 2:4) When I think of how good God has been to me, I just want to say to God, "I am so sorry for my sins. Please forgive me." That's what repentance is -- admitting you have sinned and wanting forgiveness. God has been good to you if you will just look around. Perhaps some of you are like me -- a survivor. God has brought you through incredible circumstances. You could have died or should have, but God in His goodness and mercy brought you through your trials. Accept His love in Christ. We are all sinners. Like God said, *"For all have sinned, and come short of the glory of God." (Romans 3:23)*

He will forgive you because He gave His life for you on the cross. He is alive and will come into your life if you will only ask Him to save you and forgive you. *"That if thou shalt confess with thy mouth the Lord Jesus, and shalt believe in thine heart that God hath raised Him from the dead, thou shalt be saved... For whosoever shall call upon the name of the Lord shall be saved." (Romans 10:9,13)*

Perhaps you could pray a prayer like this:

Dear God, I know I am a sinner. I believe you are so good to send your Son, Jesus, to die on the cross to save me. Please forgive me; I am sorry. I ask you to save me, forgive me, and take me to heaven when I die. I trust you alone for my salvation. Thank you for being so good to save me. - Amen.

Top to bottom:

1. John Bishop
   4th Grade

2. John Bishop
   6th Grade

3. Cold Springs
   Elementary
   School where John
   attended during
   grades 3-6

Top to bottom:

1. The home John first lived in from 2nd to 6th grade on Holston Lake in Bristol, Tennessee

2. John Bishop as a junior in high school in 1969

3. John Bishop played wingback for the East High Patriots 1969-1970. He was a captain on the team.

Top to bottom:

1. Goose Pimple Junction, Virginia, John preached here in Bethel Baptist Church for six months as a senior in high school. This was the only store in town. The town had a population of twenty nine.

2. Evangelist John Bishop after graduation from Bible college in 1973.

3. John and Donna Bishop were married in 1973 at First Baptist Church, Morrisonville, Illinois.

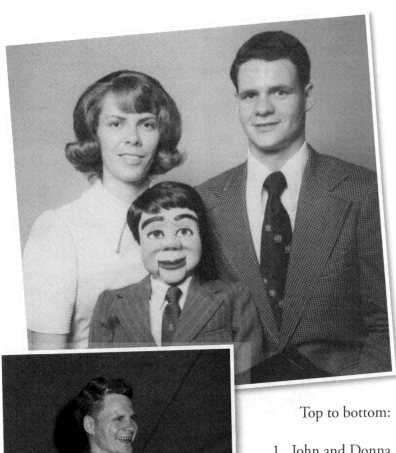

Top to bottom:

1. John and Donna with our first child, Timmy (Dummy) 1974

2. John preaches at Triple "S" Christian Ranch in the 1980's.

Top to bottom:

1. The Bishop Family in 1989 (left to right: David, Donna, Luke John, and Mark)

2. John on his scooter. This was the only way he could drive after his illness for about five years.

John with
Dr. Lee Roberson

John and Donna
pictured with
Dale and Shirley
Montgomery,
the pastor who
married them
the first time
and then again
after John lost
his memory in
1997.

John pictured with his four-wheeler. His transportation around
the camp.

A Closing Word from Dr. Eric Capaci

God has truly blessed the "God Is So Good" ministries through Dr. John Bishop. The Lord Jesus has used Dr. Bishop's illness for the furtherance of the Gospel. It is astounding to think of the thousands of lives that have been touched through the infirmity that the Lord has allowed to be placed into the life of my dear friend, whom we affectionately call "Brother John." The "God Is So Good" ministries have grown through Brother John's extensive traveling, the publications division, and also his "Yes Clubs" to the students in the public schools of America.

As pastor of the Gospel Light Baptist Church, I am also excited about the ministry that Brother John started thirty-one years ago at the Triple "S" Christian Ranch. This past year, the Gospel Light Baptist Church had the privilege of the Triple "S" Christian Ranch becoming a ministry of our church. It is an honor to be the camp's pastor. I attended the Triple "S" Christian Ranch for the very first time in the summer of 1979. For the next five years, I sat on the front row approximately thirty-five times and heard Dr. Steve Roberson preach messages under the tabernacle. I know that I could say that many, if not the majority, of the decisions that I made that molded my life were made at the Triple "S" Christian Ranch. For this reason, I am so excited about being able to be involved in the camp ministry at Triple "S." The camp is growing by leaps and bounds, and I believe its greatest days lie ahead. Brother John is still the director of the camp, and his son Luke is the assistant director. The three of us, along with an awesome camp staff, will keep the emphasis where it started thirty-one years ago with salvation, separation, and service.